PHILOSOPHY AND RELIGION

PHILOSOPHY AND RELIGION

THE LOGIC OF RELIGIOUS BELIEF

JOHN WILSON

LONDON
OXFORD UNIVERSITY PRESS
NEW YORK   TORONTO
1961

Oxford University Press, Amen House, London E.C.4

GLASGOW NEW YORK TORONTO MELBOURNE WELLINGTON
BOMBAY CALCUTTA MADRAS KARACHI KUALA LUMPUR
CAPE TOWN IBADAN NAIROBI ACCRA

PRINTED IN GREAT BRITAIN

CONTENTS

PREFACE

THE PRESENT interest in the logic of religion and its claims to truth seems to me to offer an excellent opportunity for philosophy to prove its worth outside the academic field. Such interest will survive, presumably, so long as people are sufficiently sane and reasonable to be concerned with unemotional things like logic and truth, and sufficiently excited and awed by life to be concerned with something as momentous as religion. Although it is by no means certain, and should never be taken for granted, I do not think it is over-optimistic to believe that this interest will in fact persist for a long time: perhaps indefinitely. Certainly I hope so: for though there are many different views about religion and truth which are wholly sane and rational, the view that they are unimportant is not one of them.

In attempting to bridge the still horrifying gap between professional philosophers and the general public, I shall probably say much that is dissatisfying both to ardent philosophers and to ardent believers. This is inevitable; and I can only hope that I am right in supposing that an approach to the subject by one who is an amateur in both fields may be useful, at least to other amateurs.

I should like to thank Mr. Basil Mitchell for his helpful criticism, and the Rev. Noel Davey for permission to make further use of some material which first appeared in my *Truth of Religion*, published by the S.P.C.K. in the 'Seraph' series.

CHAPTER I

THE RELEVANCE OF PHILOSOPHY

EVERYBODY knows that religion has something to do with
faith, and that philosophy has something to do with reason.
These are truisms. But many people also talk as if faith and
reason were two opposed and mutually exclusive methods of
discovering truth. Such talk is indeed common and plati-
tudinous; but it is not truistic. For it is not true.

Most of us, at one time or another, have entertained in our
minds some such picture as this: We are in doubt about what
to do, or what to believe. Two different parts of ourselves are
pulling us in different directions: two voices are calling us to
follow different paths. One is the voice of Reason, the other
of Faith, or Intuition, or Inspiration. ' Do you see those
mysterious gleams on the distant hills? ' says Faith: ' come
with me and I will lead you to them: they are glimpses of the
eternal light of truth.' ' Are you sure? ' says Reason, a
sophisticated, disillusioned fellow: ' I should wait a minute if
I were you. Think how often you've been deceived in the past.
You don't want to make a fool of yourself, do you? ' Or
perhaps our voices are more down-to-earth: perhaps we have
Common Sense on the one hand, and Instinct, Hunch or
Lucky Star on the other. ' Psst! ' says Hunch: ' there's gold
in them thar hills! ' ' Aw, don't take no notice of that crazy
old man,' says Common Sense.

Under the influence of Faith, perhaps it seems to us that the
light on the hill-tops is indeed a distant gleam of the eternal
light: fixed by the glittering eye of Hunch, perhaps we believe
that there is really gold in the hills after all. But then again, after
listening to the sophisticated Reason, we begin to wonder
whether perhaps it is not simply the last gleams of the setting
sun; and we remember that the probability of there being
gold in the hills is, as Common Sense points out, very small.
We are distracted, and do not know which way to turn. We

feel that if we stick to Reason and Common Sense we may be missing something important; on the other hand, if Faith and Hunch happen to be misleading, we do not want to make fools of ourselves. Some of us choose the one party, and others the other: but there are few of us who would not welcome some sort of reconciliation between the two.

Religion has to do with faith, because it involves some kind of commitment. Making a journey to distant hills either because you believe that the light of eternity shines on them, or because you believe that there is gold in them, is the result of committing yourself to these beliefs; just as placing a bet on a horse may be the result of committing yourself to the belief that it will win, whether the belief derives from a careful study of the horse's form, or simply from a hunch. In certain respects you have faith in the hills, and faith in the horse. Or, again, you may feel nervous when travelling by air for the first time; but later you come to have faith in the pilot and the crew, and commit yourself to their care, confident in the belief that they will enable you to arrive safely. You can commit yourself to all kinds of things, and in all kinds of ways: to a belief or a statement, to a way of life, to a set of moral principles, or to a person.

Some of these commitments may seem more reasonable than others. It seems reasonable to commit yourself to the pilot of a reputable air-line company, but less so to commit yourself to a long journey with only a very slender chance of finding gold at the end of it, unless you happen to be fond of adventure for its own sake. To many people, religious commitment appears more like the second than the first; and hence arises the notion that faith and reason are somehow necessarily opposed to each other, that one can make faith-commitments or reason-commitments, but that one cannot include both faith and reason in the same commitment. Yet it is obvious that many of our every-day commitments, such as our trust in the air pilot, are wholly reasonable: that the objects of our faith are worthy, reliable objects: and that there may be good reasons for committing ourselves, even if we cannot state those reasons. How is it, then, that religious commitment and religious faith seem to be opposed or ir-relevant to reason?

It may well be that religious believers have taken un-necessarily critical views of reason or have used the word in too narrow a sense; and also that non-believers have dis-missed religious faith out of hand as unreasonable, without giving it a fair chance. But this is only a superficial explana-tion. It is more important to notice that in our understanding and assessment of religious faith we are, and have always been, in the position of children or amateurs. Almost all educated people hold a great many common-sense and scientific beliefs, and a fair number of moral principles, in common; and our comparative unanimity and agreement in these fields contrasts sharply with the prevailing lack of agreement about either the value of religious faith or the truth of religious belief. It is fair to say, therefore, that we have hardly started to learn whether or not religious faith is ever reasonable. We are as children, wondering whether we really ought to trust our fathers when they tell us that the world is round, and won-dering also how we could ever find out about it: or we are amateurs in psychology, wondering whether the psychological experts really are experts and hence trustworthy, and how we would set about finding out whether there was any-thing in their odd-sounding theories about the Id and the Super-ego.

Yet though we are children and amateurs in our under-standing and assessment of religious faith, many of us hold such a faith with a whole-hearted and thoroughly adult firmness: and some of us who hold official positions in re-ligious organizations are supposed to have some kind of professional status in expounding and clarifying it. There is thus a big gap between our ability to assess religious com-mitments and our actual making of such commitments. We feel inclined, therefore, to fill the gap by a further reliance upon faith, a bigger or a more intensive commitment: or perhaps even by trying to substitute faith for assessment and understanding. Just as children, when they feel uncertain, are told ' Trust Father ', or as doubtful amateurs are told *accomplish little ?*

'Trust the experts', so those of us who make religious commitments are told to have more faith, when we doubt the value of our commitments or the truth of our beliefs.

It is by no means necessarily unreasonable to intensify our faith in this way. Plainly ' trust father ' or ' trust the experts ' is often the best possible advice we could give to people. But we can see how we come to form this picture of an opposition between faith and reason, because of the former's extreme importance to us in certain situations. A child's own reason may make him think the earth is flat : only by faith in his father or some other authority may he accept that it is round. Thus we might feel tempted to oppose his reason to this faith, and say that he should follow the latter. We could add, moreover, that only by following faith could he arrive at the truth—not only about the shape of the earth, but about all the other things which his reason is inadequate to compass. Or to take a rather different example, we might say that the appreciation of great music depended on our having faith in it, and in those who claimed merit for it : so that, though at first it might seem to us little more than a meaningless jumble of sounds, it would later appear to us that it held certain wonderfully real qualities—provided that we were prepared to accept its merits on trust and suspend our agnosticism. Here too we might want to contrast the approach of trust or faith in the music, or commitment to it, with the approach of reason which will accept nothing that cannot be demonstrated.

But this contrast can be very deceptive. We can, if we like, oppose our ' reason ' (in the sense of being able to give reasons, or provide evidence or proof) to our faith, our trust, or our commitments. We can similarly oppose ' common sense ' to ' instinct ' or ' logic ' to ' intuition'. Yet this opposition is unhelpfully neutral as regards what is, surely, our chief interest : namely, whether on individual occasions it is right, reasonable, legitimate or justified to make commitments of various kinds. Of course it often is : the child trusting his father about the shape of the earth, the woman trusting her instincts about a prospective suitor, even the successful gambler backing his hunches, are all placing trust in something that may well be

sometimes our faith is wrong

trustworthy. But often it is not. And since we do not want to make fools of ourselves, we have to find out which is the case.

This process of finding out is, certainly, a reasonable process. That is, it involves balancing various considerations, weighing evidence, and assessing the grounds for choosing one thing rather than another. It is essentially not an arbitrary process; and if we engage in it, our choices of commitments should not be arbitrary, as with a man who says, ' To the devil with the evidence : I don't care whether this is trustworthy or not, I shall just trust it.' Such a person we should call unreasonable : and I think most of us would use the word, rightly, as a word of dispraise, by way of criticizing the person concerned. For though some of us may have little use for logic, or proof, or ' reason ' in the narrow sense, nearly all of us think that our choices should be reasonable, justifiable, and if possible right. But these words only have meaning in relation to this process of balancing considerations, weighing evidence, assessing grounds for belief, and so forth. A reasonable choice is precisely a choice for which good reasons could (at least in principle) be given : a justifiable choice is precisely a choice which could be justified by giving reasons or quoting evidence for it. Of course it is both logically and psychologically possible for a person to reject this process, together with these words to which the process gives meaning. But it would be very hard for such a man to maintain this position consistently in real life : most of us are far too well aware of its value to cut ourselves off from it deliberately. In any case, discussion, argument, or any kind of reasonable assessment is wasted on such a person, since it is precisely this process which he rejects.

Putting this in a rough and ready way, therefore, we may say that though faith may sometimes be necessary as a way of acquiring experience, otherwise unavailable, which may be useful to us in making our assessments, it does not replace or stand in opposition to these assessments as the ultimate arbiter of our choices and beliefs. Faith and Reason should not be competing for the same job. A man may need faith in great music if he is to assess it properly, just as the suspension of disbelief may help one to assess great poetry : but they do not replace the assessment so much as form a part of it. Again, once our assessment has been made it may be of far greater practical value to us to intensify our faith rather than repeat or enlarge our assessment. The enlightened but nervous air traveller would do better to try to build up in himself a feeling of confidence in the pilot than continually to rehearse the laws of aerodynamics with which he is already familiar, but which do little to ease his mind. But here again his faith does not compete with his assessment : it supports it.

There are two errors, then, which we have to avoid. The first is the error of thinking that all our commitments and beliefs must be backed by Reason if they are to be respectable, in the sense that their value and truth must be proved or shown to be certain, and that we must ourselves be able to argue convincingly for them. For there are many reasonable beliefs which do not satisfy these conditions. The mother who knows her son is innocent, despite the weight of evidence piled up against him, cannot prove the truth of her belief, nor argue for it convincingly in a court of law : yet because she knows her son, the belief might be reasonable and indeed right. The second is the error that we can dispense with Reason when we like, in the wider sense that we need not bother about whether our commitments and beliefs are reasonable or justifiable in any way at all. The mother who knows her son is innocent has a belief which is, in fact, reasonable and justifiable, and for which there is evidence of a certain kind, even if it is not legal evidence. If this were not so, we should endeavour to change her belief because it would not be justifiable.

We cannot, then, insist that philosophy can have no relevance to religion simply on the grounds that philosophy deals in reason, and that religious faith can have nothing to do with such transactions. For though we do not think that we should all be very clever reasoners, we do generally think that we should all be reasonable; and if philosophy has a part to play in helping us to be reasonable then we should attend to it, even though we do not all have to be philosophers in a professional sense. This conclusion holds even for those who appear to profess a thorough-going irrationalism in their religious commitments or beliefs; and it is an important conclusion to establish, even though it may seem rather obvious, since without it we can hardly proceed further.

But do we need philosophy to help us to be reasonable about religion? After all, we manage to be reasonable about prospecting for gold, placing bets on horses, travelling by air, learning to appreciate music, deciding about innocence and guilt, and many other things without calling in professional philosophers. Or why should the philosophers presume to advise us? Only a very aggressive and arrogant philosopher, surely, would tell us what horses to back, whom the jury should condemn, or even, perhaps, what sort of lives we should lead. We seem to be able to behave reasonably and contentedly in every field of thought and activity without this specialized guidance; and if we do require support, we might prefer to use our friends or our psychoanalysts rather than the philosophers.

In most cases, however, we know which beliefs or commitments are reasonable, or at least we know how to find out which are reasonable even if we do not possess the actual evidence. In this position we are quite right to disregard the philosopher, and turn perhaps to the priest or the psychoanalyst for the moral support needed to put the commitment into practice, or else for help in ridding ourselves of what we know to be delusions or superstitions. But we are not in this position as regards our religious commitments and beliefs. Precisely what we do not know is whether they are reasonable or superstitious. Worse than this, we are not at all sure how to set about finding out. Not only have our various assessments failed to reach any agreed conclusions, but we suspect that our very methods of assessment are unsatisfactory. We have already mentioned our child-like or amateur status in regard to religion: and this same fact, which as we have seen tempts some of us to throw over reason altogether, because it seems so far to have failed us, also points to the absolute necessity of using it. If a problem is difficult and important, we should redouble our efforts, not admit defeat.

One of the uses of philosophy—perhaps the most important use—is to clarify methodological problems : that is, to make clear how we should set about trying to answer certain questions. We do not need a philosopher when we are thinking of prospecting for gold, because we either know or can easily find out how to assess the chances of there being gold in the hills, how to detect it if it is there, and so on : we need a mineralogist instead. We do not need a philosopher if we are arguing about whether Mars is inhabited : we know how to decide this question well enough—it is simply a matter of collecting sufficient evidence. But there are some questions which we do not know how to set about answering ; and these are philosophical questions, in the sense that philosophy has a part to play in answering them. There are some commitments and beliefs about whose reasonableness we are in doubt, not so much because we lack evidence for them, as because we are not sure what is to count as evidence and what is not, or because what is commonly quoted as evidence seems ambiguous.

Religious commitments and beliefs are notoriously of this kind : however ardently we may believe or disbelieve, it is plain enough that the assessments which we make as individuals are not publicly accepted amongst all intelligent people. What counts as evidence for the believer does not count as evidence for the non-believer : and the reasons which the non-believer puts forward for dismissing religion do not seem to be reasons at all to his opponent. Consequently we need philosophy. It is important to realize, moreover, that we do not need any particular philosophy, such as those associated with Marxism, Roman Catholicism, Darwinism, etc. : we do not need a set of principles, beliefs or doctrines to absorb. We may arrive at such principles later, but meanwhile it would be not only misconceived but dangerous to begin with them. For it is between these sets of principles, and other sets, that we may have to choose : obviously, therefore, we cannot assume the truth or value of any of them before we start. We need a kind of philosophizing that is logically prior to any of these : something that will enable us to carry out a more fundamental assessment.

This is not necessarily to say that making this assessment is going to be a very complicated and difficult business. If questions of metaphysical truth and falsehood arise, as I believe they must arise, then we are likely to need all our philosophical powers; but we cannot simply assume that this is the position. Thus it might be true, as some people think, that choosing a religion (or choosing between having a religion and not having one) is a matter of taste : logically similar to, though no doubt psychologically more important than, choosing between dry and sweet sherry, or choosing between drinking any kind of sherry and not drinking it. In that case, deep questions of truth hardly arise : the most reasonable thing to choose is the thing you like best, the thing which suits you, or the thing which will give you most satisfaction in the long run. The philosopher's job would end with making this clear; then we could either turn to the psychologist for guidance about what would give certain individuals the most satisfaction, or simply leave the matter open for people to choose for themselves. The philosopher's role would be the purely negative one of showing that this choice was no more than a matter of taste.

If we are to approach this subject reasonably, therefore, we have to avoid not only taking sides, but also making philo- sophical assumptions which may not be true. Not only must we drop our specifically Catholic, Marxist, Freudian, or vaguely agnostic points of view, but we must also drop any assumptions we have about the nature and claims of religion. We do not yet know whether religion is concerned with truth at all, or, if it is, whether ' truth ' is used in its usual sense, or indeed whether in fact there is more than one sense of ' truth'. We are not sure whether it involves commitment to a set of hypotheses, to a person, to a set of moral prin- ciples, to a general outlook on life, to the practice of certain ritual at regular intervals, or to a mixture of these. It is philosophy's first task to clarify such matters.

Its second task, which is closely bound up with the first, is to make clear those grounds which we would accept as reason- able for making whatever commitments are involved in religion, to elucidate the logical nature of these grounds and clarify their logical status. As a result of an investigation of this sort, philosophy may be able to make at least an indirect recommendation : a recommendation of methodology. It might be able to give advice about what sort of reasons are relevant to our assessment, what kind of evidence it would be worth our while to collect. Thus we now know, largely as a result of a long history of trial and error, that if we want to establish the reasonableness or otherwise of scientific beliefs, we should adopt the method of observation and experiment, and that introspection and ' armchair science ' are comparatively unhelpful. Despite an equally long, and far more painful, history of trial and error in religion, no publicly-accepted progress seems to have been made, which suggests that our methods of assessment are basically at fault ; and it is possible, if optimistic, to believe that philosophy may be able to save us from further confusion and anxiety.

The lack of a method of assessment which is publicly agreed and accepted—let alone the lack of agreement about the conclusions of any such assessment—lays rather more obligation upon both believers and non-believers than perhaps they are willing to accept. We say that we ' know ' that the earth is round or that stealing is generally undesirable : these views are ' justifiable ', we have ' good evidence ' for them, we can ' legitimately ' ' be certain ' of them. But we also use these same words—' know ', ' justifiable ', and so on—in reference to our particular brands of religion or irreligion ; and though our usage is perhaps correct, our position is much weaker. For in the first case we can point to standards of evidence and reasons which are publicly acceptable, acceptable to any sane and unprejudiced person ; whereas in the second we can only point to those standards and reasons which are accepted by those who think as we do about religion, a group which may form a very small minority of sane and unprejudiced people. We may feel tempted to say that those who do not accept our reasons are insane and prejudiced : but this is to monopolize the words ' sane ' and ' unprejudiced ' for our own propagandist purposes. In fact we know quite well that many able and unprejudiced people are Roman Catholics, Marxists, agnostics, atheists, Muslims, and so forth. This should make us resist the temptation to claim that any brand of religion or irreligion is *obviously* the most reasonable: for ' obviously ' is partly defined by the sort of thing that few intelligent people would be in doubt about. It should also make us somewhat less ready to claim ' knowledge ', ' justification ', ' good evidence ', and so on: for although this claim is satisfied by our own standards, it cannot be satisfied by public standards, since there are no public standards.

It seems, therefore, that if philosophy is needed for reaching some agreement about the assessment of religious commitments and beliefs, we should confess it to be not only relevant but essential. For the position is not simply that it would be rather nice if we could all agree, for friendship's sake, and that meanwhile we can be quite secure in agreeing to differ: it is rather than none of us have the right, as rational beings, to feel over-secure in any of our beliefs and commitments at all. It may be, of course, that religion is only a matter of taste: in which case I should here be stressing an obligation that did not exist. But the militant and evangelistic behaviour of both believers and non-believers suggests that this would not be an acceptable view to many people. In face of the lack of public standards of assessment, it may or may not be psychologically desirable that people should choose one version of belief or unbelief and hold fast to it, for the sake of their peace of mind : but it is certainly not desirable that they should hold so fast to it that they cannot let go, even for a moment, for the essential task of viewing it objectively from a philosophical point of view.

Unfortunately it often happens that real and living interest in some subject goes only with militancy and prejudice; and conversely, that when prejudice is lessened public interest flags also. Nobody, I take it, would wish to return to the days of religious wars and persecutions : but the opposite danger of falling into an apathy which is more unprejudiced because it is more uninterested is equally real. Whatever the value and truth of religious commitments and beliefs, it should be unnecessary to point out their importance to everyone. We can do justice to them only by whole-hearted co-operation in undertaking a basic philosophical assessment in the interests of all parties.

CHAPTER II

THE CLAIMS OF RELIGION

WHAT is it to have a religion, and what is the characteristic feature of a religious commitment? Many critics have written as if there were single, simple answers to these questions : as if there was only one necessary and sufficient condition to be satisfied for calling something a religion, and one basic feature common to all commitments deserving the term ' religious '. This view is common not only to intellectuals, whom we notoriously suspect of trying to over-simplify problems of this kind, but also to ordinary people. Thus one hears remarks like ' That isn't a religion, it's just a moral code ', or ' just a way of life ', or ' just a lot of ritual ', or ' just wishful thinking ', or even (more commonly amongst intellectuals) ' just a kind of pseudo-science '. In this way people commonly try to monopolize the word ' religion ' to suit their own theoretical or practical purposes.

Yet it is true, of course, that there are certain conditions which a thing has to satisfy if it is to be properly called a religion : our use of the word does have boundaries, even if they are blurred. We all know well enough, for instance, that Christianity is a religion, as are Buddhism, Islam, Greek polytheism, and so on. Most of us would agree that we should only call Communism a religion by a kind of metaphorical extension of the word, in order to draw attention to certain qualities which Communism and religion had in common— dogma, devotion, a ritual language, and so forth. This is rather like talking about the ' social hierarchy ', where ' hier- archy ' is not used in its strict sense. A more interesting case is that of Epicurus's beliefs : he held that there might be gods, but that they had no concern or relevance for human life. Would this be a religion, even if we firmly committed our- selves to belief in gods of this kind? I think not. On the other hand, Hinduism and Confucianism are certainly religions,

though their gods might seem to us far obscurer figures
than those of Epicurus. Such considerations suggest that the
task of analysing religion rather than particular religions is
likely to lead us astray.

Most religions, however, do share four common features:
or at least, they appear to do so to the external observer. First,
they include certain beliefs, or what look like assertions of fact
which are intended to convey true information: that there is
a God, he is of such-and-such a kind that his Son was born
as a man, and so on. Second, their adherents tend to accept
some sort of authority: the Church, the Koran, the words of
Christ, etc. Third, their adherents have some kind of moral
feelings, or profess a certain way of life, and a certain attitude
and behaviour towards their fellow-men: to love them, forgive
them, treat them as brothers, and so on. Fourth, they tend to
practise certain common forms of ritual and worship: such as
being baptized, facing the east when praying, or eating bread
and wine in a consecrated and formalized fashion. It is
sufficiently well-known that different religions and sects lay
different stress on one or other of these features. Thus,
Byzantine intellectuals of the late Roman empire stressed the
first, Roman Catholics stress the second, Quakers the third,
and Pharisees the fourth: though this is not to say, of course,
that they do not (at least in theory) regard other features as
equally important.

The first of these forms a necessary, but not a sufficient,
condition for religion. It is not sufficient, since as we have
seen it is satisfied by the Epicurean beliefs, which are not
religious. They are not religious, because Epicurus's gods are
no more than a sort of scientific hypothesis: there may be
gods, he thinks, just as there may be men on Mars, but they
have nothing to do with us. What is lacking is belief in gods
who are somehow relevant to human life. This shows also
that not every belief or assertion satisfies this condition.
Communism entails plenty of beliefs and assertions, which are
also highly relevant to human life. But they are not religious
beliefs; and the best we can do at this stage by way of ex-
plaining why they are not is to say that they are not beliefs

about a God or gods, or about the supernatural. Since Communism satisfies all the other three conditions, it is plain that such beliefs form a necessary condition.

The second feature, though it is almost universally found in religion, is neither necessary nor sufficient. Suppose a man to become convinced, purely as a result of his own inner experiences, that there is a God, and that God is highly relevant to his life and behaviour. He might refuse to join any church or sect, accept the authority of any person or sacred book, or indeed any authority at all : yet we could still say that he had a religion, so long as he retained his belief in a God who (according to his profession, at least) influences his way of life. It would be possible to say, I suppose, that he accepts God's authority, inasmuch as he attaches importance to him in reference to his own behaviour : but this sense of ' accepting authority ' seems so wide as to be almost useless. Therefore, although saying ' I accept such-and-such authority ' may be a cardinal feature of many religions (perhaps particularly of modern Catholicism), it need not be so : and these religions, if they are indeed religions, must contain other features besides this.

The third feature is certainly not a sufficient condition. Communism and humanism are ways of life, and involve specific attitudes to one's fellow-men : but they are not religions. Similarly we can have feelings of terror about ghosts, or have an exaggerated respect for money, without our being able correctly to describe those feelings or that respect as ' religious.' (Phrases like ' he worships money ' are not to be taken literally.) But this feature is a necessary condition. If somebody said ' I have a religion, but it does not affect my feelings about the world or my fellow-men ', we should rightly suspect ether that he was lying, or that he did not know what the word ' religion ' meant. We should say ' What you have is not a religion : perhaps it is a set of metaphysical beliefs, or some ritual practices which you reserve for certain sacred occasions, or something else : but not a religion.' By saying this we are not tying religion down to certain specific feelings or ways of life : we do not insist, for instance, that all religions should have the sort of morality or ethic that is characteristic of the higher religions. Primitive religions lack this, but they are still religions. We insist only upon what is obvious : that ' religion ' (unlike metaphysics or science) implies a particular type of emotional involvement. The involvement may take various forms, which we will shortly discuss : but it must certainly affect one's feelings towards the world and mankind.

The fourth feature is neither necessary nor sufficient. A man suffering from obsessional neurosis may have many elaborate rituals, but not a religion : so it is not sufficient. Again, a man may believe in God and follow a great many principles which involve his emotions and moral feelings without engaging in any ritualistic practices whatever : so it is not necessary. We may suppose ritual to be used to express, or enhance, the other features of religion : thus it may be of great psychological interest, but does not here concern us logically.

We are left, then, with two necessary conditions for religion : beliefs or assertions about the supernatural, and certain feelings or a way of life. We may add a third : that the two should be connected. Epicureanism, as we saw, satisfies both conditions separately, but fails to be a religion because it does not satisfy them both together : for Epicurus's morality derives from quite other sources than his belief in the gods. When conjoined in this way, these two conditions also become sufficient ; and we may say, therefore, that if a man commits himself to beliefs and assertions about God or the super-natural, and also to a morality, a way of life, or a set of principles which is somehow connected with these beliefs and assertions, then he has a religion. It does not seem to matter very much whether we add that he must also practise to some extent this way of life, or whether we are prepared to say that he has a religion merely by virtue of professing it. It is, I think, logically possible to believe in a religion without ever prac-tising it : but in fact it is sufficiently rare for us to neglect it.

Plainly our next task must be to determine how these two essential features, the belief and the way of life, are connected. Here we must distinguish three quite different questions :

   (i) What is the psychological connection between the two?
  (ii) What is supposed (by religious people) to be the logical connection between the two?
 (iii) What is, in fact, the logical connection?

Although these are different questions, it is probable that their answers will shed some light on each other; and though the first is perhaps a question more appropriate to history or anthropology than to philosophy, we may hope that to begin by trying to answer it will turn out to have some value. At least it may do something to clarify the two essential features we have mentioned.

We must remember that undue concentration upon highly-developed religions such as Christianity may mislead us about the essential psychological nature of religion. In the higher religions we have the end-products of a long process, which probably began as soon as man appeared on this planet. In these end-products we are able to distinguish fairly sharply between an imposing and highly sophisticated structure of metaphysical belief on the one hand, and a set of advanced moral principles on the other. It is likely that this distinction was not made at all in earlier stages. Because of our present conceptual framework, it is hard for us to describe these stages accurately. We can imagine, however, that at one stage, perhaps the earliest, men were the subjects of an undifferentiated feeling towards the world, an emotional, almost personal, involvement in it, during which they regarded the features of the world and the forces in it as people rather than as objects. To use Buber's terms, they had an ' I-Thou ' rather than an ' I-it ' relationship to it. If these features and forces were not precisely people, at least they had wills : they could be offended, placated, welcomed as friends or shunned as enemies.

This attitude was a mixture of belief and emotion. If we consider for a moment a typical phrase of a primitive stage in religion, such as the Latin ' numen inest '—' there is something supernatural in there '—we can perhaps see how this phrase both states a belief and expresses an emotion. The speaker thinks and asserts that something supernatural is

he also feels awed, fearful, and abashed. We can also
re precise about the kind of belief and the kind of
emotion which are involved. The belief is essentially a non-
scientific belief, in the sense that it is not a belief about objects
or things. The primitive savage may believe that his god
controls the thunder and lightning, and this may be part of
his religion; but it would be a mistake to suppose that he is
just indulging in false theories about the causes of thunder
and lightning—that his belief is just bad science. It is not
science at all. It is a belief in personal or semi-personal forces,
which (he thinks) it would be a mistake to approach scientifically: that is why most primitives resist a bluff, hearty
scientific approach to their religion. Whatever the belief is
about, it is about something essentially queer, unpredictable,
and frightening: something more powerful than himself,
which he can at best only partially control. So too the
emotional involvement is not like other emotional in-
volvements. It is not wholly like the emotions we experience
in personal relationships between equals: nor yet like the
attitude of the poet or nature-lover. For in both these cases
we feel basically safe and secure: we are not (or not always)
confronted with that feeling of powers outside ourselves which
engenders the awe and terror of the religious man. The Latin
' religio ' is not misleading inasmuch as ' religion ' implies
some kind of binding or compelling force recognized by the
believer: something which induces in him that specifically
religious attitude which we call ' worship.'

The distinctions with which we are now familiar soon began
to appear. Certain specific things, days, places, actions or
other parts of life are 'religiosus': and by implication other
parts of life are not. ' Numen ' is not everywhere. Hence
arise specific beliefs, differentiated from the primitive awe,
and ultimately a mature theology. Similarly, as the forces in
the world become familiar, and man gains more control and
security, his feelings towards objects and things become
detached from the basic religious feeling. Certain objects will
still retain ' numen,' though they may ultimately degenerate
to the status of symbols: and certain occurences or forces

which are still not understood or accepted will remain within the scope of religion; but much of the feeling is likely to be diverted towards people, partly perhaps because people are more difficult to control than things. Religion will then still dominate one's feelings about oneself and other people: and from this it is an obvious though a considerable step to a mature morality.

The river of morality flows from many sources: but we can single out at least two sources in religion. The first of these derives from the ritualistic element. Certain things are taboo: certain actions are enjoined. Whether this is done directly, as it is in the Ten Commandments, as the orders of a clearly-defined and supreme God, or whether the feelings behind it are more vague, there is still the notion of a command or at least a necessity imposed from without on the individual. It is this which, in point of psychology if not also in point of logic, distinguishes morality from expediency: and it is plainly analogous to the basic religious feeling, inasmuch as it is essentially non-scientific and recognizes some kind of superior force which obligates or binds the individual to certain types of conduct. Utilitarian ethics, in effect, seeks to dispense with this feeling, at any rate so far as it affects our attempts to decide rationally about conduct: it seeks to dispose of morality as a separate and distinct way of feeling, and to assimilate it to rational study which more nearly approaches science, or at least social science. Such ethics are essentially optimistic, humanist, sophisticated and irreligious. Here again we see that we are likely to be misled by phrases like ' a way of life ', ' a set of values ', etc.: for these phrases represent something which is highly sophisticated and developed. Psychologically, moral rules, derived from ritual and what are felt to be externally-applied imperatives, are more basic than ' principles ', ' values ', or ' ways of life '. How far these rules themselves, and the ritual, derive from subjective feelings of guilt and fear we need not here enquire.

The second type of support which the religious feeling gives to morality also assists morality to retain its non-scientific character. Religious feeling resists the tendency to regard men as logically similar to things : a tendency which grows as science (particularly psychological science) advances further. Briefly, there are a number of concepts peculiar and essential to morality, which clash (or appear to clash) with the notion that men, like things, work by cause and effect, are capable of scientific investigation, and are ultimately to be studied by the same methods as those which we use to study things, though no doubt with more difficulty. If men's actions are all ultimately explicable in a normal manner, and in principle at least capable of prediction, doubt is cast on these moral concepts. Among those which become dubious are the notions of guilt, responsibility, blame, praise, punishment— and ultimately, justice. The religious and moral concept of ' free will ' also appears to be challenged. For, in fact, we do still regard men in a very different logical light from that in which we regard things. We do not praise a man's moral actions in the same psychological way as that in which we praise the smooth running of a machine. To our minds, a man is ' responsible ' for a murder in a different sense from that in which a bullet is ' responsible ' : the man is ' guilty ', whereas the bullet can only be called ' guilty ' by a metaphor. We might say, perhaps, though this is crude, that orthodox morality depends on a picture of a sort of inner man or self, who is essentially mysterious and unpredictable : the person's ' soul ', or his ' will '. This inner man is inviolable, and not acted upon by causes : it is not just another part of the machine. It is a kind of incarnate will, that can *do* right or wrong, rather than merely *go* right or wrong. Hence we can blame, praise and punish it (or him) according to its merits or deserts, according to justice. All this, of course, is immensely helped by religious belief : the belief that men are basically mysterious, have (or are) souls, and so on ; and this is why religious believers tend to be horrified by the scientific approach to the human personality.

It is here necessary to repeat our warning against being misled by the kind of language which one has to employ in analysing the connection between belief and morality in religion. We must distinguish between what actually goes on in the minds of religious people, and any attempt to clarify or analyse this logically or psychologically. Thus it is difficult to avoid conveying the impression that believers have given conscious assent to the points brought out by our analysis : that they have, for instance, *decided* to adopt an ' I-Thou ' relationship towards the world, or *chosen* to use a scientific approach towards some things and a non-scientific approach towards others. Indeed, it is only in one sense that people choose a religion at all. Religion usually either grows on them, or overtakes them suddenly. St. Paul did not decide anything on the road to Damascus, either before or after his sudden conversion, and though this may be considered an extreme case, it is in general true that people do not weigh pros and cons before they enter on religion—or if they do, it is usually not the balance-sheet resulting from the pros and cons that actually motivates them. In the same way, though believers may argue their morality from their religion, such argument is done after the event : so far as the mental state of the believer goes, belief and morality are both part of the same attitude. A Buddhist may say ' We ought to revere all life, because all life is divine ', but this is an argument of a sort which he uses either to convince other people or to try to revive a feeling of reverence for life in himself. His own attitude is not properly expressed by ' divine, therefore to be revered ', but rather by ' divine-and-to-be-revered '.

This in turn should make one beware of the descriptions of moral thought given by modern or sophisticated writers, whose prime concern is with the logic of ethics. We have already noticed that any kind of utilitarian ethics, which represents moral thinking as a matter of means and ends arrived at by rational calculation, fails to give a faithful psychological picture of religious morality. The same is true for any analysis in terms of ' criteria ', ' principles ', ' standards ', or ' desirable states of affairs '. It is also true of the logically illuminating point brought out by recent writers on ethics : that our particular moral views are ultimately a matter of our own choice or decision, and not a matter of scientific proof. For it is psychologically false to imply that most people make a conscious choice or decision about their moral values. They either acquire, or retain from childhood, a certain attitude towards specific actions or motives : and it is this attitude which alone characterizes moral issues, as distinct from issues of expediency or taste. For the actual content of morality may vary from society to society : it may include actions like eating beans, walking more than a certain distance on Sundays, marrying your deceased wife's sister, or wearing skirts which do not cover the knees. It is true that certain actions, such as killing, stealing and lying, form part of the content of morality in most societies : but it would be quite possible to conceive of a society which did not have moral feelings about such actions—indeed there are plenty of occasions in civilized life where these feelings are suspended, as for instance in war. It is also true that certain ethics, such as the Christian, may be interpreted as opposed to this distinction between issues over which we feel morally, and issues which are matters of expediency or taste : as when a Christian might say, ' The whole of life is sacred.' But this is not an attempt to deny or devalue moral feelings : it is an attempt to extend them to cover other issues besides those which we now consider to be moral issues. Moreover, such attempts are nearly always unsuccessful : morality remains distinct, backed by its own distinct feelings. From this point of view the discourse of deontological ethics more nearly represents the state of mind of those engaged in moral thinking : though this is not to say, of course, that such ethics provide the best analysis of the logic of morality, or recommend the best methodology for solving moral problems.

At bottom, therefore, belief and morality in religion are psychologically homogeneous, being compounded of the same attitude to life. How religion develops will depend on local conditions. It is possible for a religion to be unduly weighted either on the side of belief, or on the side of moral feeling, and it is probable that most successful religions or religious revivals succeed by uniting or reuniting the two elements. In certain forms of Buddhism, for instance, the moral attitude is so dominant, to the exclusion of belief, that we sometimes hesitate about using the term ' religion ' at all; whereas, were it not for the sort of evidence we have from the Greek tragedians and the mystery religions, we might be tempted to think it possible for a classical Greek to entertain beliefs about his many gods without any serious feelings of awe or terror.

Psychologically, then, religion arises from the encounter of our own fears and desires with the world, which gives rise both to assertions about the world and to certain feelings in ourselves. Whether there is anything in the world which can be the proper object of these assertions we are not yet in a position to say: we do know, on the other hand, that men tend to adjust their beliefs to fit their fears and desires. In other words, it is psychologically probable that their feelings have moulded their beliefs: the sheer variety of beliefs is itself sufficient to vouch for this. The psychological connection between our two essential features is thus largely clear: the beliefs largely depend on the feelings. Whether they do, or must, entirely depend on them is still an open question.

But this will not do as an answer to the second question, the question of what is supposed (by religious people) to be the logical connection between belief and morality. This is not a hard question, and I think there is no doubt at all that religious people claim to derive their ways of living and moral principles from their religious beliefs and assertions about the supernatural. ' God is love, *therefore* we must love each other ', ' Christ was his Son, *therefore* we must follow him ', ' Those who die gloriously in religious warfare go to Paradise, *therefore* fight bravely ', and many other statements, all show quite clearly that believers suppose their principles to be logically reinforced by supernatural facts. ' Certain things (of a supernatural kind) are so: therefore act thus ': that is a generalized form of the whole of what religion has to tell us. This point is unaffected by the endeavour on the part of some believers to use morality itself as evidence for the existence of God. For, first, it is not a particular set of moral values which are used but the alleged existence of objective moral values as a whole: believers do not first decide on their particular morality, and then adjust their concept of divinity to fit it—or if they do, they do not do so deliberately, which is the present point. Secondly, the existence of a supernatural and objective set of moral values is itself a matter of belief and not of morality : so that the attempt is, in fact, to use one metaphysical belief to point the way to others, and not to derive judgements of fact from judgements of value. Thus, to Kant, ' the starry heavens above and the Moral Law within ' are both facts which point to God. As soon as we get to particular principles, the movement is always from what God is like, wants, or commands, to what human beings ought to do.

The third question is a little more complicated. How, actually, could a way of life or a set of principles ' derive ' from a set of assertions or beliefs about the supernatural? It is generally recognized that no amount of statements of fact necessarily entail any statement of value or any moral principle : that one cannot strictly deduce a way of life or a set of principles from a set of factual assertions. Thus, it does not directly follow from ' God is love ' that ' we ought to love each other.' We should have to include another premise, the statement that ' we ought to act according to God's nature ', or ' we ought to do what God does ' : and these are statements of value or moral principles. Even this addition might seem insufficient to some of us. Most Christians believe that God judges men, but that we ought not to do so. So we should have to start making exceptions to our general rule to act as God acts. If these principles are derived from assertions, then, they cannot be logically derived by deductive reasoning.

Nevertheless it is plain that the assertions might be logically relevant to our way of life, provided that they are relevant to our chosen ends. ' Those who die gloriously in religious warfare go to Paradise ', if we assume also that ' we want above all things to go to Paradise ', would obviously affect out attitude towards being killed in battle. ' If you do not accept the authority of Christ you will go to hell ' is relevant in an even more obvious manner : only a pedant would demand that the tacit premise ' you do not want to go to hell ' should be expressed for the sake of logical neatness. It is important, however, to draw attention to these tacit premises. One might believe in gods whose behaviour one did not want to follow—gods whom one thought to be evil. Within the framework of such a religion, ' the gods want me to do such-and-such ' would be a reason for *not* doing it. The fact that most religions depend for their moral principles on the idea of a good God—even perhaps defining goodness in terms of his will—is simply a contingent fact : it is not a logical necessity.

There is nothing unusual in this derivation of moral principles from assertions about the supernatural : that is, nothing logically odd. It is in this sense that the principles and decisions of most people are derived from facts, whether or not they are religious. The only difference is that in the case we are considering the alleged facts are of a peculiar kind : what we might feel tempted to call ' supernatural facts '. The reasonableness of this ordinary process of allowing one's way of life, principles, or decisions to be affected by factual considerations, therefore, demands no special defence in reference to religion. Plainly, *if* it is true that by not accepting Christ's authority we shall go to hell, and *if* we do not want to go to hell, then it follows that (other things being equal) we ought not in our own interests to reject Christ's authority. So far from being irrational, this type of argument could almost stand as a model of what a rational way of thinking is like.

Yet this logical connection between beliefs and principles, between assertions of fact and assertions of value, would be of academic interest merely unless we had reason to suppose the beliefs and assertions to be true, or unless we thought that it was reasonable to commit ourselves to them. It turns out, then, that the reasonableness of religious commitment stands or falls by the reasonableness of commitment to religious beliefs and assertions of fact. Here it is important to remember that these beliefs and assertions form a necessary—perhaps the most necessary—condition for religion. Whatever kind of beliefs and assertions they are, whatever kind of truth they are supposed to hold, whatever is the appropriate method for verifying them, and whatever the actual evidence for or against them, they must be genuine beliefs and assertions, in the sense that they must be logically capable of allowing

C

us to derive a way of life or a set of principles from them : for if they are not, not only are they themselves in suspicion, but also the connection between them and their derived offspring is fatally severed. And this severance would be a death-blow to anything that can properly be called a religion.

Various critics have interpreted the logical nature and status of these beliefs in many different ways. Some have thought that they act as stories or myths designed to give psychological reinforcement to our ways of living or our principles, verifiable within their own context much as statements about the characters in fictional novels are verifiable, but without necessarily having any reference to external reality. Others claim that they are like parables which, while not precisely asserting facts about the supernatural world, nevertheless provide us with useful analogies in reference to it. Others again hold that what seem to be religious assertions are hardly assertions at all, but are more like certain types of poetry, giving us an insight into reality and a special kind of truth. To others, they appear merely as a closed system of assertions, the terms of which are comprehensible only in relation to each other, but which does not necessarily have meaning or reference in respect of other assertions or other experience : a system which we have to swallow whole, as it were. Yet others might point to the ritualistic nature of religious language, claiming that its sentences are easier to analyse by their use rather than by their meaning : much as an introduction such as 'To His Most Excellent, Serene and Exalted Majesty, High Potentate, Omnipotent and Victorious . . .' has an obvious use, but may actually assert little. Such interpretations as these, and many more besides, have been and are being used to give an account of religious belief.

In making such interpretations the critics are trying to answer the question 'How is religious language used?' or 'What is the logic of religious assertions?' In answer to this question, many of the interpretations may be highly illuminating : we might even go as far as to say that one or more of them were right. But there are two other questions to which such answers might be less illuminating, or indeed largely

irrelevant. First, ' What must these assertions be like if they
are to sustain the fabric of anything which we would want to
call a religion (as opposed to wishful thinking, a reinforced
outlook on life, a poetic vision, etc.) ? ' ; and second, ' What
do religious believers think to be the logical status of their
assertions? ' Thus, suppose we interpret religious assertions
as reinforcing myths. From the objective and philosophical
point of view this may be very plausible. But then, first, a
disinterested onlooker might say ' If that's what Christian
assertions are, then I shouldn't call them religious assertions :
either you've missed the point, or else Christianity isn't a
religion. In either case I'd be more interested if you analysed
genuinely religious assertions, or else showed that there were
no such things ' ; and secondly, a religious believer might
say ' Sorry, but that just isn't the sort of thing I'm trying to
assert at all : I simply do not intend to assert myths or stories.'
Of course the philosopher may reply to the first ' Well, in that
case I should say that there weren't such things as " genuine "
religious assertions, in your sense ' ; and to the second ' Very
well then, perhaps you or somebody else can tell me what you
are trying to assert, since I have tried my best and failed.' But
we would still be left with the feeling that he had *explained away*
religious assertions ; and though this may be the only thing
you can do with them, there is a chance that our dissatisfaction
is well-grounded. So long as there is a chance, we shall be
interested in it above all else. Philosophers may be able to
show that religious believers give every appearance of asserting
myths, expressing poetic visions, etc. rather than stating facts
about the supernatural ; but this would make the religious
believer try some other way of stating facts, so as to avoid
giving this deceptive appearance, and would be unlikely to make
him give up trying to state facts at all. Only if philosophers
can show that it is in principle impossible to do what
believers try to do, that it is logically futile to make the attempt,
will the interest in religion on the part of unprejudiced on-
lookers flag, or the desire on the part of believers to make
genuine assertions grow cold.

No doubt those who make these dissatisfying though not

necessarily unsatisfactory interpretations do so because they suppose, perhaps rightly, that it is fruitless to ask for ' genuine ' religious assertions in the above sense, and that it is a waste of time for religious believers to try to make them. But it is also worth while pointing to one ambiguity which may be partly responsible. If we ask what the use or function of a statement is, we may be interested in either or both of two things : the intention or purpose of the person who makes it—what he is trying to do with it—or the job it is actually doing. For example, if a man says ' All men are equal ', a philosopher might be able to show that this functioned as a statement of value, not as a statement of fact. The man might then say ' Oh yes, I see now, I was indeed trying to express value and not assert fact—the factual appearance of my statement was misleading.' But he might say ' No, I quite understand that my statement does seem to function as an expression of value, but I do not intend it as such : that isn't what I'm trying to use it for. I'm using it to express a fact, though it may be hard to see what sort of fact, or how one would verify the statement.' In order to do justice to this position, we should at least have to be careful in our rather sweeping talk about ' the use ' of the statement. For in considering communication, it is important to remember that it is primarily people who use statements : statements do not exist abstractly for the benefit of analytical philosophers.

Perhaps the following parable may help. Imagine a man scooping around in the water with a sieve. A critic observes him and says, ' Aha, that's a sieve he's using, though he may not know it : he won't get any water up with *that*.' He taps the man on the shoulder and tells him so, saying ' My dear chap, you're using a sieve. Now the use of sieves isn't to scoop up water : it's quite different. You may not have observed that it's a sieve—the holes are rather small—but I happen to have keen eyes, and I assure you all the water is running through the bottom. Come now, you don't *really* want to scoop up water at all, do you ? You just want to watch it trickle through the bottom, or else you think the exercise is good for you,' But the man answers, ' Thank you very much for letting me know.

I suppose a lot of people would use it as a sieve, now that you mention it. But I'm not just playing a game with it, and I'm not scooping up water either. I'm trying to scoop up lumps of gold ore and precious stones, and it serves the purpose quite well. I don't often find them, but there's nothing wrong with the instrument I'm using. I'm sorry if you don't believe in my gold ore and precious stones—perhaps we could discuss that later : but you mustn't dismiss them just because I use a sieve to scoop them up.' The sieve, of course, is the assertion of the believer, which could not scoop up any ordinary empirical facts (water), although it might seem to be doing so. To the critic the assertions look like serving a quite different purpose, such as telling stories, reinforcing moral principles, etc. (letting the water trickle through, taking useful exercise). But in fact it might be scooping up something valuable and real : the gold and precious stones of religious truth, which are just as real, just as much composed of matter, as water is— only they differ in quality.

I am not here arguing that the above parable represents the true situation : as regards this, we have proved nothing yet. But I am arguing that it might, logically, do so : and that nobody has yet shown that it does not : and also, perhaps, that it would be very difficult for anybody to show any such thing. Since the chief interest of the ordinary man would (rightly) be devoted to what *he* takes to be the use of religious assertions, just as it would be devoted to whether there were in fact any lumps of gold or precious stones, it seems worth while to give serious attention to this point. There is also the dissatisfaction of religious believers to consider : for it is an undeniable fact that the great majority of such believers, even when they fully understand the philosophic interpretations of religious language which we have mentioned, would feel that they wanted to say more than the philosophers would have them say. For this reason also, it seems to me that the most important task of the philosopher of religion is to see how their claims could—even if only in principle—be made good.

For this reason we are not bound to undertake a thorough survey and analysis of religious language. Such analysis would be bound to be incomplete, and it would be likely to be misleading in an important way. The concept of ' normal usage ' offers at least a starting point, and perhaps a touchstone, for the philosopher of non-religious language : but I doubt whether the concept has any cash value in religious language. Much religious language is technical, in the sense that it can only be fully understood in its context : but religious words do not have the strict and approved definitions which apply, for instance, to technical terms in science. This is a double difficulty. Moreover, different religions, and different people within the same religion, use religious words and language in different ways : so that it is usually fruitless to ask what the usage is in any case, unless we know who is using it. Thus, one's understanding of the word ' God ' is chiefly assisted by knowing the religion of the speaker, and the speaker himself. It is fortunate, therefore, that we need only make a rough division between different types of religious assertions as they seem sometimes to be used : our prime object being, not to see how they are used—an almost impossible task—but to see what sort of usage is required to sustain the fabric of religious truth, in the way which we have found to be necessary.

We can distinguish four groups of assertions :

(i) Assertions of empirical fact : e.g. that there was a man called Jesus, who lived in Palestine in the first century A.D., who was crucified, who died, and who (in some sense) lived again after death.

(ii) Analytic assertions, or assertions concerned with the meaning or use of religious terms : e.g. that a sacrament is an outward and visible sign of an inward and spiritual grace.

(iii) What look like assertions of empirical fact, but whose subject-matter appears to be some supernatural entity or state of affairs : e.g. that there is a God, that the man called Jesus was his Son, that we shall live on in another world after death, and so forth.

(iv) Assertions of value : e.g. that it is wrong to work on the Sabbath, or that we ought to love all men as brothers.

Having made this brief analysis, we must add another word of warning. For in noticing that few assertions have a fixed logic—since one person may use a statement as analytic, and another as empirical—we have noticed only one difficulty. A further complexity is that many assertions are mixtures, in the sense that they include terms appropriate to more than one category. Thus 'Jesus lived in Palestine in the first century A.D.' is purely empirical : but ' The Son of God lived in Palestine in the first century A.D.' is a mixture, for reference is made to the supernatural. Again, ' God is good ' mixes supernatural and ethical terms : and we might further note that this particular assertion may be used analytically—that is, goodness may be conceived as something which can be predicted of God by definition : it might be considered nonsense to say 'God is not good.' It is very difficult to single out any assertion which has an unambiguous logic in the eyes of all believers ; but so long as it is clear that there are these four types of logic, this hardly matters.

On which of these should we concentrate our attention? Not, surely, on empirical assertions. It is not these which are peculiar or essential to religion. Nor would they, in themselves, provide us the stout framework for religious truth which we are seeking. This is true, however much Christians, for example, want to say that theirs is a ' historical ' religion, or ' is founded upon the historical fact of the Incarnation'. For the Incarnation (if it is a fact at all) is not *only* or even primarily a historical or empirical fact. The only empirical fact (in a strict sense of ' empirical ') is that there was a man called Jesus, born in Palestine, etc. etc. ; and nobody would have much interest in this fact, were it not also asserted that this man was God—and this is not an empirical assertion in the sense that it does not deal with ordinary facts in the natural world. Assertions about the supernatural would no doubt be of diminished interest to religion if not conjoined with empirical assertions, but they would still be of interest : whereas empirical assertions, if not conjoined with any assertions about the supernatural, would be of no religious interest whatsoever.

Similarly, although I do not want to question the great

value to religious beliefs of definition-statements or statements about the use of words, such as ' a sacrament is an outward and visible sgn of an inward and spiritual grace ', and although it is obvious to anyone with a reasonable knowledge of religion that our understanding of the use of any one religious term depends very greatly on the way in which it fits into the general terminological framework, religious language would not be interesting from the point of view of our present enquiry if it consisted wholly of a closed logical system, comprehensible only in terms of itself, and without any reference to any reality outside itself. Theology would then be little more than the playing of a magniloquent logical game, according to rather elastic rules. There would be no special reason for anyone to play the game : so that religion cannot depend primarily on such statements, which must rather be regarded as useful tools, much as the technical terminology of science is useful, for the exchange of concepts and the general flow of verbal currency within a system which must itself be firmly founded on fact.

Finally, we can reject assertions of value as a basis of religious truth, for reasons which we have already discussed. However much men's values and principles may, in psychological fact, influence their religious beliefs, it is apparent that they cannot logically be used to make them true. No apology is necessary for repeating this important distinction. It may well be that the greater part of most religions is composed of a moral commitment or outlook projected into a supposed supernatural, and that religious beliefs are really convenient crystallizations and bulwarks of such commitments. But this does not exonerate us from the task of discovering whether the logic of religion *must* necessarily work like this. The fact that most believers, in my view, would reject such logic supports our enquiry.

I conclude, therefore, that the religious claims in which we should be chiefly interested are those assertions which appear to express ' facts about the supernatural'. (This is a vague phrase, but it will do for the present.) Perhaps we may remind ourselves that this concern is highly relevant from the standpoint of the sociologist as well as from the standpoint of the logician or philosopher. For it is upon the retention or abandonment of just these beliefs that the retention or abandonment of religion as a whole depends. The beliefs in the supernatural are psychologically as well as logically primary. As has happened in the last fifty years in this country, and in most other countries which depend very much on science and industry, it is these beliefs which are the first to go, if religion is declining. Parents who have abandoned them may still teach their children a religious way of life, or sets of moral principles cashed out of religious capital: but they will be unlikely to teach them the beliefs in such a way that they will be permanent and enduring. Teaching a child to believe in God just because it is nice for the child to have something to believe in is a short-term policy that will not pay very good dividends: teaching him to believe because the belief is true, and showing him why it is true, might be a much better long-term investment—if it is possible.

CHAPTER III

RELIGIOUS ASSERTIONS AND TRUTH

A. Some theories about Religious Assertions

I WANT to begin this part of our enquiry by considering a number of philosophical theories about the logic of religious assertions, theories which are not only fairly popular to-day but which have been current in one form or another for many centuries. Unlike the interpretations at which we glanced in the last chapter, these theories try to do full justice to religious assertions, in the sense that they purport to show that these assertions are genuinely factual and to explain how their logic makes this possible. This, together with their popularity, would alone make it well worth our while to consider them in some detail; and there are also two other good reasons for doing so. First, although in my opinion they fail to provide religious assertions with a logic in virtue of which they are genuinely factual, they nevertheless have a great deal of light to shed on the way in which religious language appears to be used, and in which arguments about religion proceed: and this, though not the chief task of our enquiry, is certainly highly relevant to it. Second, we may perhaps be able to see, by considering what I take to be the defects of the theories, precisely what logical backing must be given to religious assertions if they are to be genuinely factual.

1. *Assertions as explanations*

Perhaps the most common view about religious assertions—outside strictly philosophical circles—is that they are required to fill in, as it were, the gaps left by science. It is felt that science does not tell the whole story: it omits some things, perhaps something that is inherent in the whole structure of reality, something which alone makes science itself possible. The supernatural obtrudes itself, either into particular features of the natural world or into the natural world

as a whole; and religious assertions explain these
intrusions.

Various versions of this view have been and still are widely
held. The least sophisticated version, but perhaps still the
most popular, is to the effect that the assertions explain certain
facts given to us in our everyday experience—ultimately
perhaps by our sense-experience—which would otherwise be
unexplainable. A standardized form of religious defence
appears in the question ' How else do you account for so-and-
so? ' Some feature of the supernatural world (usually God or
a god) is brought into play in order to account for some features
of the natural world. At earlier stages of religion this defence
was invariable: thus, thunder and lightning would be offered
as signs of the existence of Jupiter, fire falling from heaven
upon the altar as a sign of Jehovah, and so on. Naturally this
sort of talk looks rather obviously anthropomorphic: the
ancient Greeks and Hebrews seem to us to be reducing their
gods to the same logical level as men, even if they are super-
men. But when we remember that most people's conception
of the supernatural is far more crude than most intellectuals
suppose, we may suppose that we have not advanced very far
from anthropomorphism: indeed, we may only have a more
sophisticated version of it.

It is usually only certain particular features of the natural
world which seem to call for a supernatural explanation.
Amongst these we may list miracles, like the dividing of the
Red Sea before the Israelites: sudden changes of heart or
conversions, such as the conversion of St. Augustine or of St.
Paul on the road to Damascus: lives believed to be of extra-
ordinary (or we might significantly say, ' superhuman ')
virtue and piety, like that of St. Francis of Assisi: and the
apparently miraculous order and beauty of the natural world.
To these we must add, not a feature of the natural world, but
its whole existence, which is frequently quoted as a reason
for believing in a Creator, on the grounds that it is otherwise
unexplainable.

We may observe that these all share a common characteristic: namely, they are all unusual. Miracles, dramatic

conversions, saintly lives, and the existence of orderly and beautiful worlds or universes are not things we meet with every day. Moreover, they are all things which appeal to our imagination: they strike us with awe, wonder, and delight. It is for these reasons that we feel tempted to invoke the supernatural as an explanation. There would surely be something odd in invoking the supernatural to account for phenomena like the tides of the ocean, the falling to the ground of unsupported objects, or a man's particular liking for peppermint creams, and though we might want to say that God sends the lightning and the thunder, hurricanes and floods, we should not normally want to say, in this context, at least, that he is immediately responsible for the rather unexciting, everyday weather which we experience most of the time.

Now this is rather odd, because we are actually ignorant of the explanation of many of these everyday phenomena; and even when we have a rough idea of the sort of causes involved, we cannot explain or predict them fully. Our ability to predict the weather is strictly limited, at least in certain regions: and it would be very hard indeed to give any kind of plausible explanation of a penchant for peppermint creams. It appears clearly, then, that we do not go around invoking the supernatural whenever we cannot lay our hands on a natural explanation. We only do so when the phenomenon is striking and unusual, as is often the case with psychological phenomena, which we find less easy to explain than physical phenomena owing to our comparative lack of progress in psychology. This looks rather suspicious.

Let us suppose that we are savages, and believe that God is responsible for the ebb and flow of the tides. A civilized scientist comes along and explains to us that these are actually caused by the gravity-pull of the moon and the geographical configuration of the world's oceans and land-masses. Probably we shall accept this explanation in time, and think that we were fools to have been so superstitious. But we might say ' Ah yes, I see now how the tides work, by gravity, land-masses, etc. But this doesn't destroy my belief: it's still God, working through these things, who is responsible for the tides.' In much the same way, certain cures of physical diseases were thought to be miraculous : we said ' God did it.' If we now know how the cures were worked, we may say ' God didn't do it, the doctor just happened to use the right drugs by good luck, or it was just that the nurse gave him baked beans for tea—the one thing which, as we now know, can cure such cases.' But we may also say ' Ah yes, all this is so, but God still cured the man, working through the minds of the doctor and the nurse.'

In this way we see that this theory has two lines of defence. Either we say ' There are some things science can't explain ' and invoke God to explain them, or (if this defence is penetrated by a proffered scientific explanation) we say ' Science can explain them, but that doesn't show it wasn't God too.' Now the first line of defence can be invalidated in two ways :

(a) There might be a natural explanation for these phenomena, in the sense that our present scientific knowledge, or a slight extension of it, might be able to cope with them if we knew some more facts. Thus, however striking it may seem to us that St. Paul was converted, it might be that a slight extension of psychological knowledge would fully explain his conversion, and that a psychologist possessed of this knowledge could have predicted it at the time. Such knowledge might have nothing to do with God, but be concerned with psychological concepts such as the Super-ego and with features of St. Paul's life, such as his ill-health. There is no special reason why we should affirm that every phenomenon must, in principle, be amenable to scientific explanation ; we might say that this was a creed or a working hypothesis rather than a proven truth—though the fact that scientists have explained a vast number of phenomena suggests that the creed is a very reasonable one. But certainly there is no reason to affirm that science cannot in principle explain any particular phenomenon : it is very hard to see how this statement could be supported at all. In fact, we do not normally give up trying to find a scientific explanation for striking cures or other miracles, just because they are striking or miraculous : we do not use the name of God as an axe to cut short the advancement of our understanding.

(b) Suppose that we did decide that we could explain a phenomenon by reference to God. In finding an explanation for something, we usually carry out experiments in order to test which factors in the general situation are responsible for the phenomenon and which are not : and the acid test of the validity of our explanation is usually the test of predictability. Now by saying that God is responsible, we appear to be saying that there is a factor (which we call God) which must play a part in our explanations and predictions. In other words, we appear to be offering ' God ' as part of a scientific hypothesis, which might be the rival of some other hypothesis. Thus, a sceptic might say that the Red Sea divided because of some natural phenomenon, such as an unusually strong wind : the believer might say ' No, it wasn't a strong wind, it was God.' This may seem naïve : but it is a kind of argument with which we are all familiar, and which sufficiently displays the sort of mistake which believers are likely to make in taking this line. The mistake is that if God is really offered as part of an explanatory hypothesis, as a strong wind might be offered, God is reduced to the level of a natural feature : perhaps a feature which we had not previously recognized, and which we now have to take into account, but having a logical status similar to other features. God becomes simply one cause amongst others ; and so far as the theory which we are considering goes, there is no reason to call this cause supernatural. In other words, as soon as we fit features of our experience into a scientific pattern of cause and effect, they shed their mysterious and supernatural quality : they become natural features, however striking the results which they may produce.

If directly challenged as to whether they wish to regard God as simply another cause, most sophisticated believers would probably deny it : though I do not think this is true of believers in general, particularly those in a less sophisticated age than our own. To most people, God acts like a person : he may be more powerful and more mysterious, but his actions are still logically similar to the actions of people in the natural world. ' God caused it ' is parallel with ' the doctor caused it ' : they can operate as rival hypotheses. His actions may be unpredictable, but so are the actions of people. On this view, neither seem to merit supernatural status. God becomes rather like a poltergeist : something mysterious and incomprehensible, which we feel tempted to invoke in order to account for strange happenings. What occurs is that either the happenings are adequately explained by other methods, so that we cease to believe in poltergeists, or else we learn how poltergeists work, so that they become ordinary natural forces for us, and we should probably stop calling them poltergeists. So on this theory God, invoked as an explanation in this simple way, is either a myth, or merely a natural (albeit immensely powerful and obscure) force whose workings we do not grasp. It seems doubtful whether anyone really wants to accept the God which results from this. A savage might worship the mysterious force of electricity : but once convinced that it could be at least partially understood and worked into a comprehensive scientific pattern, he would probably cease to do so.

The second line of defence is also invalid ; indeed, it is fairly obviously a kind of cheating. If we say ' Yes, I understand all about gravity and mass and attraction and so forth, but I still want to say that God makes unsupported objects fall downwards', then a critic would rightly suspect either that we had not really understood about gravity, etc., or else that when we added to all this ' God makes unsupported objects fall downwards ' we were not adding anything by way of further explanation. For if we have properly understood the explanation, no further explanation is needed : the existing explanation is quite satisfactory, and the invoking of God does not make it more so—for instance, it does not enable us to predict anything more accurately. We may indeed be saying something significant when we insist on invoking God even after a full explanation in natural terms : but it cannot be anything that would help in an explanation.

This points the way, however, to a more sophisticated use of God as a kind of cause or explanation. The story is now, not that God is a cause parallel to other causes, and hence responsible on particular occasions for particular features of the natural world (like miracles), but that he is a kind of permanent background which is necessary for the working of the natural world as a whole. One could perhaps compare his status here to that of light in the natural world, which offers a permanent and necessary background to a wide variety of phenomena : or to heat, which inheres to some extent in all objects, but which we tend to overlook. Thus, just as we might say ' If there were no heat, things would not happen as they do,' we might say ' If there were no God, things would not happen as they do.' Here God operates as a cause, in the sense of a necessary condition, a *sine qua non* : something that must be taken into account if we really want a full explanation. But this conception too is open to the same attack. As soon as ' God ' is used to explain a state of affairs, either as an active and direct cause, or as a necessary condition, he is immediately being used as part of our normal processes of science. If he plays that part effectively, he is robbed of his supernatural status : if he does not, the whole point of bringing him in at all is lost.

We could try to avoid this point by supposing that God was in principle unpredictable and mysterious, so that there was no hope of fitting him into a scientific hypothesis, and we avoid the necessity of reducing his status from supernatural to natural. Could he still function as an explanation? It might seem that he could. Supposing we liken the human race to a colony of ants, and compare God to the human being who is in principle out of range of the ants' predictions and knowledge : an intelligent ant might then say of certain curious phenomena, like the pouring of boiling water over the anthill, that they were the work of a super-ant agency which could not be predicted and was essentially mysterious. The ant might also ascribe the general set-up of ant life to human agency : and if it were a semi-artificial ant-hill, erected under a glass cover and in conditions specially designed by humans for the purpose, this might be true. Pursuing this analogy, but still without bringing in God, we might imagine that the human race was in fact under the control and observation of certain super-beings of immense power and inconceivable potentialities : that the solar system, or even the whole universe as we know it, was an artificial set-up rather like the artificial ant-hill, or the animals in a specially-designed nature reserve. If this were true, it would give us both some understanding of curious phenomena—analogous to external interference by the super-beings—and a general answer to questions about the creation and sustaining of the universe as a whole.

But it is not hard to see that answers to questions of this kind in terms of God or super-beings are empty answers, and consequently cannot stand as explanations. They are empty, because they do not really give any genuine information. They do not point to new experiences, or new ways of collating our experiences into explanatory hypotheses which are of any use. We can say of any occurence ' It is the work of a super-being ' : but this is too easy. Such a statement could be interpreted as a denial of the possibility of scientific progress : it could mean ' We shall never understand this, because it is due to an agency in principle outside our range.' But it is difficult to see, as we have already noted, what evidence could be adduced in support of such a view. If it is taken literally, there is an equal shortage of evidence. It may be true that there is a God or that there are super-beings : but we cannot induce this from any occurence. All we can induce from an occurence is that the occurence has a cause : by which we mean, at least, that we shall probably be able to understand why it happens if we work hard enough. If we already know from other evidence that there is a God or a super-being, then to say that an occurence was caused by one of them becomes informative, because we shall then know something about them. Until we know something about them, to say ' It was caused by God ' is no better as an explanation than to say simply ' It was caused.'

The invoking of God to account for the whole of the natural world or universe is a kind of third line of defence. The defender admits that phenomena in the natural world are explainable by other phenomena in the natural world : but holds that if you consider the whole of the natural world—all the phenomena or things there are—and then try to explain that, you have to bring in God. But this is even less defensible. Suppose we admit that some special thing (called God) is responsible for the whole universe as we know it at present, then this thing will simply be numbered amongst the other primeval and cosmic forces which we know about, and it would be perfectly proper to try to account for its existence as well. The critical child who says ' And who made God? ' has a good point, and the pseudo-devout parent who replies ' Hush, dear, that isn't a sensible question ' is not even using God as an explanation, which is bad enough : he is using him merely as a block to prohibit further enquiry. In fact, of course, it does not add anything to our knowledge of or about the universe to say that God made it : it is certainly not an explanation. We might put this point alternatively as follows :—If ' the whole universe ' or ' everything that there is ' does not include God, then God might in principle be part of an explanation of its origins, but we should then want to ask the same questions about ' the whole universe ' in a sense in which the phrase included God. If the phrase does include God in the first place, plainly God cannot be invoked as an explanation, since he is part of what is to be explained.

Finally, we have to deal with the most sophisticated or at least the most confused version of this view. Its supporters claim that the providing of explanations as a whole, or the whole of scientific enquiry, presupposes a background of metaphysical or religious assertions which must be true. In other words, God or the supernatural order must exist, otherwise we would not be able to make sense of the natural order. Stated thus baldly, perhaps this view does not seem very plausible : but we must remember that science as a form of enquiry—particularly if you give it a capital S and make it sound grand—has tended to acquire a kind of mystic aura in the last few centuries, and that Scientists have committed themselves to a large number of statements of a metaphysical rather than a scientific nature. Thus Sir Cyril Hinshelwood says of knowledge of chemistry and its students : ' To this knowledge they attach an absolute value, that of truth and beauty. The vision of Nature yields the secret of power and wealth. . . .'[1] Einstein interprets scientific enquiry as enquiry about God : ' God, who creates and is nature, is very difficult to understand, but he is not arbitrary or malicious.'[2] Finally, and most clearly, Professor Coulson : ' For that common search for a common truth : that unexamined belief that facts are correlatable, i.e. stand in relation to one another and cohere in a scheme ; that unprovable assumption that there is an " order and constancy in Nature ", without which the patient effort of the scientist would be only so much incoherent babbling and his publication of it in a scientific journal for all to read pure hypocrisy ; all of it is a legacy from religious conviction.'[3]

We are not here concerned with whether particular religious beliefs, as a matter of historical and psychological fact, have assisted or inspired scientific investigation : though I should guess that those religions which allow the natural world to become detached and freed from that peculiarly religious awe which the world inspires in a primitive savage, rather than continue to invest it with mystery and unpredictability, have assisted science if only by non-interference. The question is rather whether the assumptions which Coulson mentions must be true, if we are to account for the success of science. Once again, it is salutary to bring the matter down to earth. Does my ability to predict that wheat will grow if I plant wheat-seeds, that heavy dark clouds are likely to bring rain, that the sun will rise to-morrow, or that if I let go of a ball it will fall to the ground, imply any metaphysical presuppositions whatsoever? Yet such predictions are not logically different from scientific predictions : briefly, the difference lies chiefly in the fact that science is more highly organized than common-sense observation, and this difference is not logically significant in the present context.

This should make us suspicious of talk about the uniformity of nature, or ' the unexamined belief that facts are correlatable'. For what does this belief amount to? It implies

[1] *J. Chem. Soc.*, London, 1947, p.1277.

[2] The words are inscribed in a room at Princeton University.

[3] C. A. Coulson, *Science and Christian Belief*, p.57.

that nature is set out or arranged artificially, like a giant mosaic, all the parts of which form a regular and intelligible pattern : whereas, it is argued, the mosaic might be purely random, without any pattern at all, so that we could not predict anything or discover any ' laws of nature'. In this simple sense of ' regular ', however, we should say that some of nature was regular and some was not : sometimes we come across a pattern in the mosaic, sometimes a pattern is lacking. It is less misleading to say that we are constantly on the look-out for regularities, in order that we may make useful predictions. Sometimes we succeed in finding them at once : sometimes we do not, and then we try harder by collecting more facts or suggesting new hypotheses. It is of course logically possible that there are some phenomena which we shall never be able to work into an observed pattern of regularity : but all our experience is against such a supposition.

For, after all, what is the belief denying? Could it be anything but true? And if it could not, can it really be asserting anything significant or giving a useful explanation of anything? Thus, it is hard to see what could be meant by saying that nature was not uniform—other than, trivially, that everything around us does not fall into an immediately recognizable and symmetrical pattern. Similarly, supposing we said that ' facts are not correlatable ', what should we mean? We might mean, I suppose, that we could never know from one moment to the next what was going to happen. But such a universe seems inconceivable : and not only inconceivable in practice and in the imagination, but logically inconceivable. If anything at all exists, it is possible to make empirical statements about it and to make predictions. For all our knowledge of things around us is based on co-recurrent experiences, out of which the very concept of a thing or an object is built up. So long as there are things, we are bound to be able to detect some regularities, just because some degree of regularity in our experience is part of what we mean by a ' thing ', and so long as there are regularities, prediction and science are possible. If this belief means anything at all, therefore, that is not trivial in this

context, it seems to mean either ' We can do science ' or
' There are things with regularities ' : and these hardly escape
from triviality. It is true that there might not be things, and
hence that we might not be able to do science—a natural
handicap under such conditions : in this sense we could say,
I suppose, that the existence of things is an explanation of
why science is possible. But it is not an explanation that brings
us at all close to religion, or to the picture of an artificially-
designed universe which this view is attempting to smuggle in.

It is worth asking why the notion of regarding religious
assertions as explanations arises at all. I believe it is a misconceived attempt to cling, at all costs, to the view that the
supernatural affects or inheres in the natural world. This
view does indeed form an integral part of the religious attitude,
as we have seen. Under the immense impact of modern
science, however, the mistake is made of supposing that the
only possible relationship between the supernatural and the
natural must be that of *explicans* to *explicandum*. In other words,
the supernatural is not clearly conceived as different in kind
from the natural. Consequently supporters of this view are
continually trying to squeeze the supernatural into concepts
which are tied down to the methods of natural science and
common sense : concepts like ' explanation ', ' cause ', and so
forth. Such methods can only do religion a disservice. They
are mistaken in much the same way as it would be mistaken
to try to explain why a cathedral stands up by reference to
its beauty, majesty or power. Whatever the relationship
between the two categories, it is much more subtle than this.

2. *Assertions as self-justified*

This view regards religious assertions as having some
reference and relevance to external reality, but denies that
any evidence can be found for them in the outside world.
They are supposed to be self-justified, as it were : to stand
solely on their intrinsic merits. The difficulty is to see how
any satisfactory sense can be given to ' self-justified ' or ' self-
guaranteeing'. For, in a strict sense, nothing can be self-
justifying, since to justify something means to give good

reasons for it in terms of something else: and the same applies to ' self-guaranteeing '.

We might say of a work of art, perhaps, that it ' justified itself ' ; but we should probably mean that certain standards of justification were inapplicable to assessing its merits, not that we had no need of standards at all. Thus we should not be disposed to rely on Aristotle's formal criteria for assessing a tragedy, but would prefer to scrutinize it carefully for ourselves, closely observing its various characteristics and its effect upon our minds. Yet this would not be to abandon standards altogether : those characteristics and that effect would seem to us relevant considerations for assessing its merits. Again, we might say that a man's trustworthiness ' declared itself ', or that we could see that he was trustworthy ' just by looking '. But here too we should mean, not that we had no external evidence for trusting him, but that we did not need written testimonials, or references, or long-continued personal experience of his behaviour, to have reason to trust him. Certain people do, no doubt, strike us as trustworthy almost at first glance ; but if our belief in them is reasonable, it is only because we have reason to think that people who do strike us in this way are, in fact, to be trusted : and this must depend on other evidence.

By its very nature, this theory does not provide us with other evidence. Various versions of it stress different features of religious assertions considered as a whole. One writer says that our decision to accept them, ' denied the aid of ready-made criteria, must be reached by a scrutiny of the thing itself; as happens, perhaps, when we judge the merit of any great and original work of art ', and again ' What is distinctive of divine inspiration must be sought in the subject-matter, the product, and the conviction of divine origin which accompanies it and which it is able to communicate '.[1] But precisely the same arguments apply. Religious assertions may give us ' a conviction of divine origin ' : but a conviction is not evidence. It is significant that the writer says that our acceptance of them is a matter of decision : we are not to

[1] Austin Farrer, ' Revelation,' *Faith and Logic*, ed. Basil Mitchell, p. 102.

weigh, calculate, search for evidence, or do any of the other things which we normally do in considering whether an assertion is true. We decide to commit ourselves, or not to commit ourselves.

This view has at least the merit of suggesting that religious assertions must be approached in quite a new way: that there is a different methodology for discovering their truth. Moreover we have a close parallel to the kind of decision-acceptance here suggested: the parallel of our acceptance of a work of art—particularly of poetry. The concept of ' poetic truth ', indeed, might be thought to give strong support to the notion of ' self-justified ' assertions, and it will be worth our while to examine it more closely.

The difficulty with this concept is that we should only want to call a statement true if it described something which was actually so: if (to put it roughly) it corresponded with the facts, or communicated to us some information which fitted some feature or features of the world. Of course other things can be true besides statements. We may say that a general's assessment of the enemy is a true one, even if he does not actually say anything: we may also say that a good map gives a true representation of the countryside, or that a painter paints a true picture of the scene before him. But what we dignify with the word ' true ' here are still descriptions, or pictures, or representations: they are things which are supposed to have a valid reference to an external reality. The general's assessment is true because the enemy are actually disposed as he believes them to be, not because it is made with the general's authority or expressed in fine language. The map is true, because the countryside is actually as represented on it, not because it is a beautiful map, hand-painted with dolphins and wind-filled cherubs. The picture is true, because the scene does actually look like that, not because of the picture's artistic merits or the painter's skilful grasp of significant form or colour.

Consider Shakespeare's ' The iron tongue of midnight hath told twelve.' Suppose I say this, not as a character in *A Midsummer Night's Dream*, but just after I have heard a cathedral clock strike twelve, at midnight. Would that be true? Of course it would be, because the clock had just struck twelve midnight. Now suppose I said instead ' The clock has just struck twelve midnight ' or ' The iron tongue of the bell in the clock has just struck twelve midnight ', if we are going to be precise about it, would this be any less true? Surely it would not: it is just as good a description or representation of what has happened. So it looks as if a prose description is just as good as Shakespeare's poetic one.

But any admirer of poetry would be discontented with this; and rightly. ' No,' he would say, ' there's much more in Shakespeare's line than in your prose version. Consider the skilful vowel and consonant sounds in the line: the bold elliptical phrase " the iron tongue of midnight " : the effective ambiguities in " told ". Your version doesn't contain any of this; and this is natural, since poetry is different from bald statement of fact.' Of course this is all true. Poetry *is* different; but not because it tells a different kind of truth. The poet's skill consists in producing a certain effect upon us, in giving us certain types of psychological stimuli. We do not know how he manages to do this, though we can point to various features in poetry—vowel sounds, ambiguities, evocative images, symbols, and so forth. But in doing it, he does not describe. We, his audience, are not receivers of information : we are receivers of stimuli. He may present us with a picture : but its merits, as poetry, will not depend on whether the picture is true to life. For the purpose of the poetic picture is not to represent, but to affect. And we may affect people by various methods—sticking pins into them, doing strip-tease performances in front of them, or telling them jokes—which need have nothing to do with truth.

This is not to say that many poets may not, in their poetry, set out to represent to the reader either what certain aspects of the world are like, or their own feelings. We are not here concerned with their own feelings, which may be purely subjective ; but it seems that if they really wished to *describe* them they would hardly choose the medium of poetry to do so : they would write an autobiography, or indulge in psychological self-analysis. This applies too to any representation of the world : if we wish to describe the world, to point out certain facts, we do not use poetry. The illusion that poetry is descriptive of the world arises from one important fact, which tough-minded critics are apt to miss : namely, that the effects which poetry can have upon us may be a very useful preliminary to our reaching knowledge of the world, and hence being able to describe it. Certain experiences may eventually lead to knowledge, even though they are not experiences of receiving information. Thus, if I wish to communicate as much knowledge as possible to other people about the problem of disease and its horrors, I might publish a health report containing a vast number of true and verifiable statements. If instead of this I simply confronted a number of people with the spectacle of a man with leprosy, so as to shock them, I should have described nothing, and said nothing true ; but I might thereby arouse their interest and give them an experience which might lead them to acquire further knowledge. This kind of emotional confrontation is not too dissimilar from the way in which some poets work : though by no means all poets.

We can thus see how, without degrading poetry in any way, we must nevertheless deny its claim to make true statements over and above its prose significance ; and we can also see how the temptation to ascribe poetic truth to poetry arises. For it would, indeed, be appropriate to ascribe other things to poetry. We could say that poetry gave us ' illumination ' or ' insight ', for instance ; and these are important things. Similarly, it might be held that religious beliefs gave us this same illumination or insight : that they provided us with certain important experiences. But could these experiences, in the case of religion, be useful to us in acquiring knowledge ? The fatal gap between the assertions of religion and the outside world still exists, and this theory does not fill it. Even if it did, this would hardly be sufficient, inasmuch as the assertions of religion are supposed to be themselves true, not merely to be psychological aids to truth.

The general force of these arguments applies not only to

the concept of ' poetic truth ', but to any notion that religious assertions can be self-justifying. It is possible to hold that these assertions do not fall within the field of descriptive language at all—that they do not describe, but do some other job : but it is not possible to hold simultaneously that they are genuinely factual or informative, in the way which they must be if they are to sustain the fabric of anything which we should call a religion. Certainly, one can use language for many purposes ; and not always to describe. Besides the evaluative and analytic uses which we have already mentioned, there are many others. One can play with language as Lewis Carroll does. One can use it to convince or persuade as do orators. One can joke with it. One can use it to create atmosphere, as in a ghost story. One can use it to exclaim, express feelings, make promises, or lay down rules. None of these uses are primarily descriptive or information-giving None of them *tell* us anything directly, though we may induce information from them on our own account. The child who says ' Ow! ', the man who says ' I promise ', the umpire who says ' Out! ', and the raconteur who says ' It was a dark and stormy night ' are not primarily concerned with stating facts. That job is done by third-party statements : ' He is in pain ', ' He promised ', ' He was out ', and ' The story-teller said " It was a dark and stormy night".'

All these, and many other uses, are self-justified in the sense that we do not need to check with the outside world in order to verify them : for checking and verifying only arise when the question of information arises. If a poem, a joke, a decision or a promise comes up for justification at all, it is justified by its effects, not by its accuracy. The reader or hearer may, in a sense, commit himself to it. He may say ' Yes, I endorse that ', meaning that it has won him over. But he does not say ' I believe that ' : for belief implies some sort of correlation between the statement and the outside world, between the set of symbols and the thing symbolized. Naturally the symbols need not be merely counters—a quick, dry way of communicating. They may have some kind of emotive connection with what they symbolize, as in poetry. Thus the poet and novelist can regenerate in our minds experiences which we have had, but have been only half-aware of having. Under such circumstances we may well be tempted to say ' How true ' : though the writer is plainly not describing, but evoking.

Moreover, it is a mistake to suppose that, whenever a symbol or set of symbols arouses our feelings or imagination, there must necessarily exist in reality something for which the symbols stand. The existence of symbols used as counters, merely for giving information, does not prove that anything exists to which they correspond, as words like ' unicorn ' and ' mermaid ' show. Similarly, though the poet or the religious writer can strike chords in our minds, and make us feel things, this does not show that he is actually writing about anything that exists. A great deal of our minds, particularly at those deep levels on which poetry falls, is autonomous, and not merely a receptacle into which experiences of real things have passed. Thus, although it is quite possible to make out a case to the effect that religious assertions are in a class by themselves, they must—logically must—either be also classified as descriptive, in which case they cannot be self-justified, or be also classified as non-descriptive, in which case they need no justification, but cannot be factual.

A more sophisticated version of this view directs our attention to religious assertions as a whole, and claims that the corpus of these assertions is self-justifying in much the same logical way as a corpus of empirical assertions is self-justifying. Both of them, as it were, stand on their own feet, and it is fruitless to look outside either corpus of assertions for justification. Thus one writer says ' One can accept religion in its own terms or reject it ; there is no way of justifying it by translating it into other terms ', adding with some honesty ' And this means, if you like, that religion as a whole lacks any justification.'[1] Another writer compares religious belief with a certain way of looking at the world : for instance, the belief that everything happens by pure chance, and says that if we believed this '. . . although we should not be *asserting* anything

[1] A. Mackintyre, *Metaphysical Belief*, p. 202.

different from those of a more normal belief, there would be a great difference between us ; and this is the sort of difference that there is between those who really believe in God and those who really disbelieve in him.'[2] (We should treat reality in a different way : not trying to explain, plan or predict anything.)

It is certainly possible to represent types of discourse (empirical discourse, religious discourse, moral discourse, and so on) as logically different games, so to speak, which one can either play or not play, and any one of which cannot be justified by reference to any other. But first, we must be careful that the games are really different. Someone who believed that ' everything happens by pure chance ' is, in fact, asserting something different from the rest of us : to say that something happens by pure chance is usually to say that it cannot be predicted or explained—and in many cases this is demonstratably untrue. To hold despite all the evidence that dons are insane, or that one's motor-car is liable to come to pieces at any moment (to quote two other examples of what this writer calls ' bliks ', or ways of looking at the world), is to hold an untrue assertion. If I hold that dons are not sane and cars not trustworthy, then the chances are that either I have not attended to the evidence ; or (if I have attended but reject it) I do not know what is meant by the words ' sane ' and ' trustworthy '. It would be like denying that it was hot when the thermometer read 100 degrees in the shade : either I have not noticed the thermometer, or else I do not know what ' hot ' means. For words like ' sane ', ' trustworthy ', and ' hot ' are tied down to public standards of verification. Similarly, if religion is to be treated in this way, it must play its own game, and avoid conflict with other games : including the game of science, where in fact it does not avoid conflict.

More important, the logical disparity and separateness of the various games does not excuse them from some kind of justification. It is not *rational* to hold that all dons are insane : and this could be shown quite apart from any proof that it

[2] R. M. Hare, *New Essays in Philosophical Theology* (ed. A. Flew), p. 102.

was not *true*. The game of moral discourse is rational, though no question of proof or truth arises in the way in which it arises in science. It is rational, because it is useful to us to value things, to make moral decisions and judgments, and so on: just as it is useful to do science. It fulfils our purposes. Justification of this kind may be an appeal to self-interest; and there is no hint in this version of the theory about how the religious game could be backed up by a rational appeal to self-interest; and indeed it is difficult to see how it could be. Even if it could, it seems impossibly remote from religion as it actually is. Believers would not be content to subject their beliefs to tests of self-interest, and give them up if they found that they did not minister to that end so efficiently as other beliefs, or no beliefs at all. Yet some such rational consideration as this is required if we want to know, as we do, whether we ought to adopt the religious ' blik '. Further, even if these objections did not hold, we still have not managed to show how religious assertions are genuinely factual in the sense required.

Part of the trouble with this theory is that it seems unaware of the dangers of cutting religious assertions off from the rest of our beliefs and experience; and it is perhaps worth noticing that its exponents often rely on a too facile assimilation of the religious outlook with other outlooks, usually the scientific. Thus Mackintyre writes: ' Of science and morals it can also be said that one can justify particular theories or prescriptions, but that one cannot justify science as a whole in non-scientific, or morals as a whole in non-moral, terms.'[1] These remarks are somewhat ambiguous; but it seems to me that some process which might be called ' justifying science as a whole ', i.e. giving acceptable reasons for accepting the general practice of science, could be given: namely, by showing how science rests—as it does rest—securely on the basis of our common, every-day sense-experience: and similarly one might, though with more difficulty perhaps, ' justify morals as a whole ' by showing that they rest on the basic facts that human beings have certain desires and purposes, and that they live together in communities. Of course it is logically possible

[1] A. Mackintyre, op. cit., p. 202.

to take no notice of common sense-experience or common desires and purposes, though psychologically it would be hard to do so ; but they do at least give us a prima facie reason for accepting science and morality. The difficulty with religion is that no such prima facie reason seems to exist at all, and it is this important dissimilarity which the smooth assimilation of religion with science fatally masks.

It would, of course, be a mistake to suppose that these theories are wholly absurd. We should say rather that they illumine some questions but not others. As a psychological description, on not too deep a level, of how believers come to believe or accept religious assertions, the notion of those assertions carrying weight because of their own form and content, and not because of their correlation with the outside world, is an extremely helpful one. Thus, it is significant that in the recitation of religious creeds or other assertions one does not adopt the attitude of someone reciting factual information. The tone of voice with which we say the Apostles' Creed is not that in which we enumerate the chief facts about the reign of Henry I, or the principal coal-bearing areas of Europe. The process is more ritualistic, more like reciting poetry : the Creed is taken as a whole and stands on its own feet. Thus the theory may be true as a description either of how believers come to believe, or of how they continue, when converted, to regard their religious assertions. But the fact that many believers can and do object to various points of a creed on the grounds that they are not true, and in this and other respects treat creeds as genuinely factual and having reference to the outside world, shows that the theory does not suffice as a complete description of their logical status.

3. *Assertions as derived from authority*

Most believers, if asked why they adhered to their beliefs as a whole, would perhaps answer that they did so because they accepted a certain authority. Ultimately this authority usually takes the form of a person—Christ, Buddha, Mahomet, and so forth—by reference to whom subordinate authorities (the Bible, the Koran, etc.) may also be accepted, and it is this

most common form of acceptance by authority that we shall
consider first.

We may assume that there must be some evidence that the
authority is trustworthy, if it is to be held reasonable to trust
him. We cannot rely on inner experiences, or intuitive insight
into his trustworthiness, for reasons already given. But this by
itself is not necessarily a stumbling block. There are plenty of
things which we believe on authority, and on reliable : though
there are plenty of other things which people believe on authority although the authority is unreliable. We may believe that
the Amazon is longer than the Thames, that aspirin is good
for headaches, and that the chemical composition of water is
H_2O. We believe that ' " Sinko " removes that sinking
feeling ', that people with certain lines on their hands will
have long lives, and that the Seventh Heaven is the Ultimate
Sphere of the Spirit. Assuming that the former are reasonable
beliefs, that the latter are not, and that we believe them all on
authority and not by first-hand experience, perhaps we can
see what distinguishes one group from the other.

First, I have good reasons to believe that the geographers
are not lying about the length of the Amazon, and that their
motives are disinterested ; whereas I am not at all sure about
this when it comes to ' Sinko '. It may remove that sinking
feeling, but it is in the maker's interest to say so anyway.
Secondly, I have good reason to believe that there is such a
science as medicine, but not that there is such a science as
palmistry : so I accept medical experts, but not palmists.
Thirdly, though I may understand neither what is meant by
H_2O nor what is meant by the Seventh Heaven being the
Ultimate Sphere of the Spirit, I have good reason to believe
that H_2O does have a clear meaning, and can be checked by
acceptable methods (ultimately by sense-experience), whereas
this is not so with Seventh Heavens and Ultimate Spheres. I
therefore accept the authority of people like physicists, but
not of people like Swedenborg.

I can, then, reasonably believe assertions of whose meaning
and verification I have no personal knowledge ; but only if
I have evidence that they do have meaning and can be verified.

I must also know that the authority who makes them is genuinely expert: I should not accept $E = Mc^2$ from just anybody, only from someone who was expert in the particular field to which this equation refers. Further, I must know that the expert is disinterested. If, then, I accept a religious personage as an authority for believing in religious assertions, I must be sure (i) that religious assertions are meaningful and verifiable, (ii) that the personage is expert in the field of religious knowledge, and (iii) that the personage is not likely to be biased or prejudiced in any way.

It is fairly obvious that we can be sure of none of these things. For (i) if we knew that religious assertions are meaningful and verifiable—by other means, of course, than taking the authority's word for this—we should be able to say, at least roughly, what they meant, how they should be verified, and what evidence there was for them : in which case we should not need the theory we are considering in order to justify them, (ii) we cannot know that a religious authority is expert in the field of religious knowledge unless we first know that there is such a field : and also we should need to check his pronouncements in this field by reference to our own findings in it ; (iii) religious personages, particularly the founders of religions, are justifiably objects of suspicion and distrust : we might well think that they were laying claim to truth in order to suit their own purposes, however high-minded those purposes might be.

I suspect that those who adhere to this theory are misled by failing to distinguish between different types or categories of trustworthiness. Whether it would be right or wrong, it would at least be perfectly reasonable to *follow* a religious personage such as Christ or Mahomet, or even to accept the moral principles and way of life taught by such a one ; but this does not make it reasonable to accept him as an authority on religious knowledge. We trust people in certain respects, not in all respects. One man I trust to repay money he has borrowed from me, another I trust to tell me about algebra, a third to guide me in my moral choices. Each of my trusts may be whole-hearted, and reasonably so. But to trust one person in every respect, without the sort of evidence we have outlined, would be accounted folly by any sane person.

Here too, however, we have a more sophisticated version of the theory to deal with. Mackintyre writes: ' Religion is justified only by referring to a religious acceptance of authority ', and elsewhere : ' What we say about God . . . we do not derive . . . from evidence, we recognize that the facts of nature and history do not provide any ground for what we say, yet we say it. Our ground for saying it is that we have the authority of Jesus Christ for saying it: our ground for accepting what He says is what the apostles say about Him ; our ground for accepting the apostles ? Here the argument ends or becomes circular ; we either find an ultimate criterion of religious authority, or we refer to the content of what authority says ', and again : ' We justify a particular religious belief by showing its place in the total religious conception ; we justify a religious belief as a whole by referring to authority. We accept authority because we discover some point in the world at which we worship, at which we accept the lordship of something not ourselves. We do not worship authority but we accept authority as defining the worshipful.'[1]

These quotations put the theory very clearly. As an account of how particular religious beliefs are verified by believers within their faith, it is highly illuminating : it is precisely by appeals to authority that this is usually done—appeals to *ex cathedra* statements by a Pope, the general tradition of the Church, early Christian saints, what a right-thinking man's conscience tells him, and so forth, are all appeals to authority. This is different from appeals to authority in empirical questions. If we are asked to believe that a certain star is 10 light-years distant, we might use an expert as a sort of check or touchstone for the truth of this belief, rather as one uses litmus paper to check whether something is acid or alkali. But the expert is not the ultimate criterion : whereas the religious authority is the ultimate criterion. One might say that the religious authority gave the belief its logical location and status : almost, that it gave the belief meaning—thus, one

[1] op. cit., pp. 200 and 202.

might answer questions about the meaning of ' charity ' by reference to St. Paul's remarks on the subject. Indeed, one might compare the part played by religious authority, in some respects at least, with the part played by the rules of mathematics. It is by reference to authoritative rules such as the multiplication tables that we verify our sums in arithmetic, and it is only by reference to the basic postulates of mathematics that any particular piece of mathematics makes sense. Here, too, it seems that one cannot go beyond these basic postulates : certainly one does not look around in the outside world for verification.

But this illustration also shows the weakness of the theory. Basically it is the same weakness that we observed in considering the ' self-justification ' theory in the last section : namely, that it gives one no kind of rational support for believing that religion is true, or indeed for believing it at all. One might say, I suppose, that a religious belief is *ipso facto* true if it is demonstrably backed by the relevant authority, just as a mathematical proposition is *ipso facto* true if it demonstrably follows from the rules of mathematics, only, I do not think that religious believers would want to say this. In any case, if one did say this, religion becomes a sort of logical game analogous to mathematics—which is no doubt why believers do not want to say it. There is nothing wrong with logical games : some, like mathematics, are empirically useful : others need not be. It remains an open question whether religion is or is not.

It may be true to say ' We accept authority because we discover some point in the world at which we worship, at which we accept the lordship of something not ourselves ' : but this is to give a kind of psychological explanation for our acceptance, not a rational justification of it. The very sophistication of the theory seems in danger of masking a vital point that must occur to every ordinary person in considering religion—the point that one can be *mistaken* in this acceptance. If one does not go through at least some kind of rational process of consideration, one may find oneself bowing down to wood and stone, like the heathen in his blindness. We would surely want to say that the heathen is mistaken on a matter of fact—that stocks and stones are not God. Even if we do not say this, we should still say (going as far as possible with this theory) that he had accepted the *wrong* authority. And as soon as we talk in these terms, we have let ourselves in for a process of rational consideration. The only possible alternative is to say that no question of reason arises: that there are no arguments of any kind which could show that a man who ' accepts the lordship ' of the devil is somehow erring, and a man who accepts God is not erring. On this view religion seems to be something which overtakes one in various forms, or does not overtake one at all: rather like a bacillus. One cannot do anything about it: one cannot even know whether the bacillus is constructive or destructive. I feel sure that any theory which entails these consequences cannot be regarded as a serious explanation of the logic of religion as a whole, however helpful it may be as an explanation of its interior logic or the psychology of religious believers.

It is instructive to see, finally, how such views as this may arise from the retention of the mythical conflict between faith and reason, which in turn arises from an over-restricted use of the word ' reason ' itself. Thus our writer envisages the possibility that ' whenever anyone denied a Christian doctrine he was at once struck dead by a thunderbolt ', of which he says: ' since the Christian faith sees true religion only in a free decision made in faith and love, the religion would by this vindication be destroyed . . . . Any objective justification of belief would have the same effect.' Elsewhere: ' There are no reasons to which one can appeal to evade the burden of decision ', and (more wildly) : ' Because it is logically inappropriate to give reasons for a religious belief this does not of itself provide a reason for not believing.' The implications of this are significant. Only a choice or decision for which we can give no justification is a free choice: we cannot use faith if we are backed by reason: it is not reasonable to disbelieve something for which no reasons can be given. But such statements sound very queer if we refer them to our normal ways of thinking and talking. Plenty of free choices can be justified : we may still need faith even though we are backed by reason : and we generally suppose the onus of proof to rest with the person who holds a belief—particularly when he is anxious to convert us. To opt religion out of the support of a specific type of reason is tolerable : but to opt it out of rationality altogether, and so to distort the meanings of words like ' free ' that they become unrecognizable, seems to me to make something very like nonsense of the whole business. Even this might be just tolerable—for it might be expected that religion would demand its own standards of rationality and its own terminology—if only it could be shown what these standards were, and what the terminology meant. And it is highly unfortunate that believers always seem to give the impression of sheering off this task. It is not surprising if some people impatiently dismiss the whole thing as irrational nonsense.

B. *Religious Experience and Verification*

It is generally easier to criticize than to construct, and in the sections which follow it is philosophically appropriate that we should feel more hesitant about accepting what is put before us. Although it is perhaps a more worth-while task to try to give a firm rational foundation for religious assertions than either to give them a false foundation or to shed a vaguely dubious mist over them, it is nevertheless a much more dangerous task. This applies particularly to any approach by way of ' religious experience '. It is popularly believed that this approach has been worked to its uttermost limits, and is now played out; hence it is philosophically unfashionable. Nor only this; for the justification of religious assertions by ' religious experience ' is alien to the general tone of this century, and particularly perhaps to western and industrialized cultures, which are based on scientific achievement.

Yet at first glance nothing would seem more natural than to try to justify assertions of fact by experience of some kind : so natural, indeed, that it seems rather naive. For it might be asked, how else do we achieve knowledge other than by our experience? All the theories which we considered in the last section refer to some kind of experience, which is alleged to be sufficient foundation for a rational acceptance of religious assertions. The first refers to phenomena such as miracles or sudden conversions: the second at least appears to rely upon the impact made by the corpus of religious belief on the observer: and the third to what seems to be an experience of authority. Why is it that these experiences do not enable us to achieve knowledge?

Briefly, it is because we do not consider just any experiences relevant to an assertion; any assertion has to be supported by certain kinds of experience only. It is this principle (whether under the name of the Verification Principle or under some other name) which in the last few decades has been chiefly responsible for casting so much doubt on religious and other assertions: not directly upon their truth or falsehood, but upon their whole logical status. The difficulty with religious assertions is that they do not seem to refer us to any specific experiences in the outside world which might be taken to support them: they do not seem, as it were, to have any lines of communication with external reality.

We might perhaps think that the experiences suggested by the theories we considered fulfilled this requirement: that religious assertions were supported by a sense of mystical conviction, the observation of miracles, and so on. But this would be to miss the point. Our choice of what experiences we take to support an assertion is not an arbitrary choice, but is dictated by what the assertion is trying to communicate to us. Thus, if I say ' There is a zebra in the next room ', only certain experiences would be taken to verify this statement: e.g., going into the next room and seeing something striped and with a long tail, hearing it neigh, feeling it bite you, and so on. Why do we confine our verification to these experiences? Because, of course, they are part of what the assertion is trying to communicate. Part of what is meant by ' zebra ' is something striped and with a long tail, that neighs and bites, therefore, if we experience these things, our experiences go to support the assertion. We cannot simply select any experiences we like, and arbitrarily hook them on to assertions: that is

putting the cart before the horse. On the contrary : we wish
to communicate that certain experiences are to be had, and it
is those experiences which ultimately back up our com-
munications. Now the experiences suggested by the theories
we mentioned do not seem to form part of the assertions they
are supposed to support. Statements about miracles, sudden
conversions, mystic experiences, trusting people, and so forth,
are not part of what is *meant* by any religious assertion. For,
first, religious believers would deny that a statement like
' There is a God ' means ' There are miracles, sudden conversions, etc.' One could press them about this, pointing out
that part of what is meant by ' zebra ' can be given by quoting
various experiences, actual and possible : they would assent to
this, but in the case of ' There is a God ' they would certainly
not assent. They would claim that our knowledge of God is
so fragmentary and distorted that miracles, sudden conversions, and so on, act as wisps of evidence, and not as part of
the logical structure of the word ' God '. To them, this claim
would be like saying that part of what is meant by ' zebra '
was ' There is a strong horsy smell, and look, something with
hooves has trodden on the geraniums.' Secondly, we can
check this by seeing how believers react if we put to them the
possibility that there were no miracles, no sudden conversions,
and so on. Of all possible reactions, one of the most unlikely
is that they would say either ' Ah, I see that there is no God
after all ', or even ' Ah, yes, I now have to change the meaning
of " God ".' Hence the link between these experiences and
the assertions seems arbitrarily forged. The gap between the
two is still unbridged.

I do not at all want to say, following on the above, that
religious assertions are either meaningless or unverifiable. The
former charge would be merely stupid, using the obviously
false assumption that only assertions which are properly linked
with experience are meaningful. Yet—to take extreme
examples—not only exclamations like ' Hooray for philosophy! ' but even vague cries like ' Oi! ' and ' Ow! ' have
some meaning ; or, if ' meaning ' is going to be narrowly
defined to suit the philosophers, we shall say that they have

some use. In any case, one decides whether a remark has meaning not by looking at it on the philosophical dissecting-table, but by seeing whether people mean anything by it (or use it for any purpose). The charge of unverifiability, in the second place, is sufficiently ambiguous for some writers to attempt, at least, to evade it. Many believers may be found to agree that some experiences count as favourable to their assertions—even decisively in favour of them—and that other experiences count against them. What is rare is to find a religious believer who agrees that certain experiences would count *decisively* against them. Of course opinions among believers vary considerably. To some, the existence of earth-quakes, disease, pain and so on count as evidence for the love of God, however odd this may seem to the agnostic : to others, they count as prima facie points against it—but only as prima facie points. For they will then set to work to explain, or explain away, these points in such a way as to retain their assertion intact. It is this process which conveys to many people, both believers and non-believers, the impression that religion is continuously retreating. Whether we are going to call assertions so treated ' verifiable ' or ' unverifiable ' is a purely verbal question : the point, which is that they are not decisively falsifiable, lies elsewhere.

One might here point out that this unfortunate impression given by religious believers, in their unwillingness to accept the full force of this principle, seems due to a desire to maintain the validity of their beliefs at all costs. Believers vary between regarding their beliefs as completely certain, and regarding them as probable. The former view is hopeless, as one can only lay claim to complete certainty (in the sense in which mathematical or tautologous propositions are certain) at the cost of sacrificing the claim that the beliefs are factual and refer to the external world. The latter is more plausible, since there appears to be no reason why we should expect certainty either way, in a matter which must surely be agreed to be difficult and dark, and about which there is otherwise very little agreement. But here too we cannot cling to a belief indefinitely, however obscure the truth. It may well be thought that no actual evidence we possess—since we may possess very little—does in fact count decisively against religious beliefs : but to act as if nothing *could* count decisively against them is suspicious in the highest degree. We can see this by comparing the situation with other problems where we are short of evidence : whether there is life on other planets, whether punishment deters potential criminals of a certain type, whether the universe is expanding, and so on. Wherever a belief is clearly formulated and understood, there it is possible—it logically must be possible—to conceive of evidence which would carry enough weight to make us abandon it.

Suppose I assert a factual belief, ' There is a zebra in the next room.' If I have had various experiences (stripes, neighing, bites, etc.), I have good evidence for the belief. If I have a great many of these experiences, it would be fair to say that I could be reasonably certain of the belief : we all know that there are plenty of beliefs about which we can be reasonably certain. But that does not mean that nothing *could* count decisively against it. Alcoholics think they see spiders crawling up walls ; and other people in abnormal states have hallucinations of hearing and touch as well as of sight. It is logically possible that I may have been given a drug which gives me a total hallucination of a zebra. If I call in other people to share my experiences—well, they might be under the influence of the drug as well. Of course this is wildly unlikely : but it is logically possible. No factual belief is logically certain : it would always make sense to deny it, even in face of the supporting experiences. There are some beliefs which it does not make sense to deny. It does not make sense to deny that zebras are animals or that squares are four-sided : for these remarks do not so much tell us facts about the world, as inform us about how to use words and concepts. It is possible to claim logical certainty for these beliefs in the sense that they are not falsifiable by any evidence collected in the outside world. But they are not absolutely certain in the sense that any such statement must, somehow, mysteriously, be true. For we might be giving wrong information about the use of words and concepts. Something *could* count decisively against these statements : for instance, a reference to a standard dictionary, text-book on geometry, etc. might prove them wrong. There is no absolute certainty in the sense in which some religious believers seem to need certainty : particularly not in the case of factual beliefs.

However, this may be merely knocking down an Aunt Sally which is by no means a feature of every religious fairground. It is more important to see how it is that experience cannot be arbitrarily tacked onto assertions. What makes the believer's claim to certainty and his consequent claim of the impossibility of decisive falsification so misguided, is his failure to perceive the relation in which verification and falsification stand to factual assertions. The Verification Principle, properly understood, is not a test arbitrarily imposed by philosophers on assertions, which they have to pass if they are to be respectably informative. It is the formulation of philosophical observation of what informative statements actually are : or if you like, of what we would normally mean by an ' informative ' statement. It is not even necessary to make the rather dangerously abstract claim that unverifiable statements cannot be informative : a claim whose ambiguity we shall have to examine later. But it is necessary to point out the relationship between verification and assertion.

Perhaps the following may suffice as a rather crude and simplified account of this relationship : I want to communicate something about the world in which we live. This world has many features in it—colours, shapes, sounds, things, etc. : not all of these are in the same logical category, but that does not matter at present. I want to tell people that something about these features is the case—that things are like this, and not like that. This I do because I or someone else has certain experiences of these features : for if nobody had experience of them, they would not be listed as features at all. Now my saying that the features are arranged in *this* way, or that things are like *this*, necessarily implies that they are not arranged in *that* way, or that things are not like *that*. (Saying that something is square is implying that it is not round.)

Now the more detailed my specification about these features, the more information I give; but also, the more vulnerable my specification becomes. For the more I want to say ' Things are like this ', the more I have to say ' Things are not like that '; and of course it may be that I am wrong, and that things *are* like that. For instance, consider the following specifications about reality, or assertions:

   (i) There is something in the next room.
   (ii) There is an animal in the next room.
   (iii) There is a zebra in the next room.
   (iv) There is a large, striped zebra in the next room.
   (v) There is a ten-foot, striped, male, lop-eared zebra in the middle of the next room.

Each of these assertions is more detailed than the last: each is more informative: and each is, in consequence, more vulnerable. It would probably be hard to upset the assertion that there is something in the next room: but a great many things could upset the very detailed assertion in (v). We may summarize this point by saying that a statement is informative in proportion to its vulnerability.

We may thus compare assertions, in this respect at least, to maps or plans. The more detailed a map is, the more possibility there is of its details being wrong. Or to use a more distant analogy, making assertions is like betting on a roulette board. We may confine ourselves to thinking only that the number which turns up will be a red number rather than a black one, and bet only on the red. Or we may bet also on the assumption that the number will be red *and* even, and place money both on the ' rouge ' and the ' pair '. Or we may take a big step and assume that the number will be red, and even, and 18, putting our chips on ' rouge ', ' pair ', and on the square marked 18. If our total wager is to come off (reversing the analogy, if our detailed assertion is to be true), all our assumptions must be right. The number must be red, even, and 18. On the other hand, if we take the more cautious policy of betting only on red, we shall win though the number may not be even, and not 18.

These analogies should also bring out a second point: namely, that the truth of assertions depends upon their being

cashed in terms of experience. Just as a bet on a roulette board
will only come off if the number and colour on which we bet
actually comes up, so an assertion can only succeed in its job
if the experiences to which it points are actually available, in
the same way as the accuracy and success of a map depends
on the countryside which it represents actually being as it is
represented. In other words, assertions must be verified by
experience. But this implies a more fundamental point : that
the assertions should be *capable* of being verified. Making
an assertion which is not actually verified is like placing
a bet on the wrong number ; making an assertion which is
not verifiable is like not putting your chips on the board at all.
If you put your chips on the side of the table, for instance,
instead of on a number, you cannot lose : but neither can you
win. For you are not betting.

Perhaps we can press this analogy still further. Suppose
that, instead of going into a public casino and using a public
roulette board, you have a private board of your own in your
own home, and place bets on it. Are you really betting in this
case, and can you win any money? The answer would depend,
I think, on whether you were playing by yourself or with a
group of friends. If you play by yourself you can put your
chips on numbers and see whether they turn up, but this is
hardly betting : you can only win money from your own
pocket, which is not really winning money. But if you play
with a group of friends, your bets and winnings are valid bets
and winnings within that group. It is true that they are not
publicly valid, as they would be if you used a public casino :
for instance, you might play according to a set of rules which
were not publicly accepted. But the rules would be valid for
you and your group ; and so would your bets be valid.

This is relevant to the ambiguity in statements to the effect
that religious assertions are not ' verifiable ', which we mentioned earlier. The question ' Are religious assertions verifiable? ' is like a question which might be asked in our
analogy, ' Are these bets valid? ' If we are dealing with publicly-accepted methods of verification (as for statements
about zebras, for instance), or with bets in a public casino,

then we have no doubt that the answer is Yes. But if we are not, we cannot answer with an unqualified No. For bets may be valid, and assertions verifiable, within a limited group. This is an important point, for there is not much doubt that religious assertions are not verifiable in the sense of being publicly verifiable—or more precisely, in the sense that there are publicly-agreed methods of verifying them. But we should not feel entitled to deduce from this that they were, without qualification, unverifiable, and hence that they could not be informative. For they might be verifiable and informative within a limited group of people. Indeed, this supposition looks rather plausible, when we remember that there are in fact a great many churches, sects, and religious groups which differ widely from each other. There are some beliefs which are peculiar to certain groups; and more than this, it is quite possible that what is (on paper) the same assertion of a religious belief may differ in meaning, verification and information from one group to another. Those familiar with religious groups would, I think, endorse this possibility.

The situation might, therefore, be like the playing of different forms of roulette by different groups of people in a community. Most forms of the game would have certain central features in common—just as most religions assert the existence of a God who is alleged to have certain characteristics, like being loving, powerful, creating, assisting men, and so forth. But there might be a great variety of local rules: the roulette board might look different, and the way of placing bets might be dissimilar, and the actual rules dictating when a bet should be successful might vary, between the groups. To someone who did not belong to one of the groups, it might be very hard to find out both the common features of the game, and also any of the local rules—particularly if the groups were not very hospitable about receiving strangers, and their members not very good at explaining the game to them; preferring perhaps to exhort them to play it with enthusiasm, rather than to describe its logical workings. So hard might it be for the external observer to understand (and not only the external observer, for the members of the groups might be able to play the game without fully understanding its logic), that he might easily conclude that it was not a proper game at all, with proper rules, but just a form of irrational entertainment, or perhaps an excuse for a social gathering. Yet he would be wrong.

Like other analogies, this shows only that group-verification is a logical possibility; and it may seem somewhat remote from the problem of religious assertions. To take a rather closer parallel, suppose that different groups of people in the world had different appreciation of colour, instead of the vast majority perceiving the same colours under the same circumstances. Obviously our assertions about colours (' This is red ', ' That's blue ', etc.) would vary from group to group. A colour-blind person would wonder whether the group members were really asserting anything about reality at all— whether the whole thing were not, as we say, ' purely subjective '. How could he find out whether there were really colours or not? To-day, of course, we have scientific tests which help us, by means of measuring light-waves, to identify each colour. But suppose we are talking about a time when such scientific tests did not exist. Then he might have to think quite hard in order to find a suitable test; but while he was thinking, each group would still be making assertions about colours. These assertions would be verifiable, though not with the scientific precision that present-day equipment enables us to attain (as thermometers help us to verify statements about heat and cold, for instance). For the group-members would share certain common experiences to which their assertions referred. Eventually the colour-blind person might hit on some such test as the following: He would induce various people to paint a large number of discs, identical in shape, size and texture, in what they claimed to be different colours. On the back of the discs he would write different numbers. He would then lay out the discs, and having noted the number on the back of one of them, point it out to the subjects of his experiment. Then he would shuffle the discs, and lay them out again. If the subjects could pick the right disc, that would be very good evidence that the disc did, in fact, differ in some way from the others : and since other differences had been excluded, this would argue strongly for the genuineness of the subjects' experiences of what they called colour.[1]

Even if nobody was actually able to think of such a test, would it be quite certain that colour was entirely subjective? Surely, it would at worst be merely an open question ; and, in fact, if anyone claimed at the time that it was subjective, he would have been wrong. This should at least make us hesitate before dismissing the possibilities inherent in religious experience as a justification for religious assertions ; and I hope that it may also help to bring out the close link between experience, verification, and informative assertions, even if by rather a roundabout method.

Despite the apparent optimism of what we have so far said, however, there are still many difficulties to be overcome before we can accept any approach by way of religious experience. One difficulty in particular is to decide on a meaning for the phrase. It is all too easy to assume that ' religious experience ', merely by its existence as a commonly-used phrase, can do all our philosophical work for us. If there is such a thing as religious experience, it may be thought, then there must be something in religion. If there is supernatural experience, then there must be a supernatural. This has only to be stated to be seen for the logical sleight-of-hand that it is. Plainly the equation of ' supernatural experience ' with ' experience of the supernatural ' begs the question. But we can see, perhaps, how the temptation to beg the question arises. We commonly talk about ' seeing a zebra ', ' hearing a bell ', and so on : and it is easy to slip from this into talking about ' having experience of a zebra ', ' experiencing a bell ', etc. Then, when some of us have rather unusual experiences, we may feel like calling this ' experiencing God ' or ' knowing God'. But we can see that even when we talk of ' experiencing a zebra ', we assume that the zebra exists. It probably does exist : but it might not, for we might be suffering from a hallucination. To be quite sure, we check our experience by others—by touch, hearing, smell, and so on. No experience by

[1] I owe this example to Professor A. G. N. Flew.

itself establishes its existence; and no experience by itself establishes the existence of God. We can only talk about ' meeting God ' or ' experiencing the supernatural ' if we have good reason to believe that God and the supernatural are real.

From this example it looks as if we shall need what might be described as a network of actual or possible experiences, such as we have with zebras : a network which acts as a kind of verification- or test-system for checking assertions that a zebra is really there. If we just seem to see it, that is quite good evidence. We might be having a hallucination, however ; so we pile up more and more relevant experiences by touching, hearing, smelling, being bitten, and so on. The more experiences we pile up, the more points are scored for the assertion. Of course we do not usually have to go through any such complicated process : we soon learn which of our experiences we can trust, and which are unreliable. Nevertheless, this is the logical sub-structure of our assertions : and in cases of doubt, it is this which we use. Hence we see that assertions do have to pass tests : not arbitrary tests, but tests which they impose on themselves, as it were, because of what they assert. Thus the zebra-assertion refers to a whole network of actual and possible zebra-experiences, to the whole test-system : it cannot be verified conclusively by a single one.

' Religious experience ', then, is a phrase which must be used with care. We may find ourselves falling into a commonly-used trap, set as follows : We are asked whether there is such a thing as religious experience. If we say Yes, we commit ourselves to accepting a special type of experience and (unless we are careful) to the existence of supernatural features or entities from which the experiences comes. If we say No, we seem to be denying that certain people have mystical, strikingly unusual, or other-worldly experiences or feelings : and this denial hardly does justice to the psychological facts. We must surely admit these facts, whilst pointing out that they do nothing to establish any sort of objective reality. ' Religious experience ' is ambiguous rather as ' seeing stars ' is ambiguous. It may be used to imply an experience of something that exists independently of the observer—really seeing luminous bodies in space : or it may be used colloquially, of people who receive a sudden blow on the head, to imply only an experience like the experience of seeing real stars. It will be safest to use it in the sense in which it does not necessarily imply objective reality.

In this cautious sense, we must surely grant the existence of religious experience, even though we may find it difficult to say what counts as a religious experience and what does not. But we accept that some people have mystical, striking, or other-worldly experiences. The evidence that they do so is not strictly the concern of philosophy, but I do not think anybody would be very much concerned to deny it. Of course we can cast cold water on it, if we like. We can say things like ' That's because you haven't been feeding yourself properly ', ' That's just because you've got a strong Super-ego ', and so on. But none of this is relevant to the logical part which such experiences play, or may play, in supporting religious assertions.

It may still be doubted, however, whether there are in fact certain experiences which we are entitled to group together under the common name of ' religious ', even if this is not taken to imply that the experiences are experiences *of* something. The implication behind the phrase is that there are different types or levels of experience, of which ' religious experience ' is one. Many philosophers would be suspicious of any such implication : it is still fashionable to use ' experience ' and ' sense-experience ' as loosely synonymous, which reflects the modern creed that sense-experience is the only sort of experience worth talking about, because it is the only sort of experience which leads to knowledge of empirical facts. Indeed, the word ' empirical ' itself, which strictly means ' relating to experience ', tends to be monopolized into meaning ' relating to sense-experience '.

In common usage we speak of all sorts of things as ' experiences ' ; being in love, seeing zebras, feeling happy, having a pain, enjoying music, and so forth. It is certainly proper to speak also of mystical or religious experience : that is, these phrases do describe something which some people feel. If we

consider the experiences they are supposed to describe,
varying from Socrates' divine voice to Wordsworth's ' spirit
that rolls through all things ' (in *Tintern Abbey*), by way of the
experiences of St. John of the Cross, St. Joan, and John
Bunyan, we may well consider the group a heterogeneous
one. But the group of experiences we call ' being in love '
may be equally so, and the phrase may appear equally vague,
yet it has its use. Our criteria for determining when we are to
use it are various : we rely partly on the behaviour of the
person involved, even though this may vary considerably, and
partly upon the description that he himself gives of his
experience.

Of course it is fairly simple to distinguish between one type
of sense-experience and another : for such experience involves
the use of sense-organs, and we can verify by scientific means
which particular organ is receiving impressions. But this is
not the only possible method of distinguishing : we have the
criteria mentioned above, which we saw to be partly be-
havioural and partly autobiographic. It is also in principle
possible that we could verify and distinguish between types of
experiences such as being in love, feeling hungry, and having
mystical feelings, by scientific methods : for instance, we might
find that different areas of the brain were active in different
cases, or we might be able to classify and explain such experiences by psychoanalytic theory. Thus it is alleged to be a
common feature of many types of experiences, including the
feeling of exaltation and other-worldliness that is often
characteristic of religious experience, that the Ego and Super-
ego are temporarily identified.

Nor need we be disturbed by the commonly-held view that
all knowledge and every kind of experience depends ultimately upon sense-experience. I do not think this view is
unassailable, unless of course it is made true by definition.
Thus the existence of extra-sensory perception might be taken
to count against it ; but if it were said that such perception
took place by means of a ' sixth sense ' or some hitherto un-
detected sense-organ, it would seem that the thesis was being
turned into an analytic principle—that any means of obtaining

knowledge was by definition a ' sense'. But, in any case, this is hardly relevant. For nobody need claim that religious or other experience is not causally dependent for its existence on sense-experience. We wish to claim only that it would be misleading to describe it as *merely* sense-experience: that it is different in kind. We can accept that Wordsworth would not have had his semi-mystical experience at Tintern Abbey if he had not had the use of his eyes, so that he could see his beloved nature: but we do not have to say that all he really experienced was a number of visual impressions. To say that one thing causally depends on another is not to say that the two are identical, or even that the first is merely a sophisticated version of the second.

C. *Objectivity and Existence*

Most people accept that there is such a thing as religious experience, and I do not think that many critics would take violent exception to the rather cautious conclusions of the last section. A far more common charge is that such experience does not indicate that the supernatural, or any feature of the supernatural such as God, really exists outside the mind of the believer. This charge is made in a great many more or less sophisticated versions. The ordinary agnostic will say that religious belief is ' just wishful thinking ', or ' purely subjective '; the philosophical agnostic that religious experience is ' not cognitive ' and cannot be used as a basis for ' existential assertions '. Both these amount to much the same thing: perhaps the simplest way of putting it is to say that religious experience is not experience *of* anything.

It is important to remember that the onus of proof in this matter lies on the religious believer, and not on the critic. We often behave as if religious belief (like the Church of England) were firmly established, so that all the believer had to do was to show the attacks of agnostics to be inconclusive; as long as religion could not be pinned down and proved false, the darts of the enemy were vain. But it is clear from what we have seen already that however firmly established religious belief might appear to be to a sociologist, it could not appear to be so to a logician. This is because we do not simply take a person's word for it, when we are considering whether experience is experience *of* anything. If he wishes to convince us, and even if he wishes to be reasonably certain that his own belief is reasonable, he has to show how his assertions are derived from his experience. Thus, if a group of people said that they had experience of unicorns, fairies, or mermaids, we might agree that they had had *some* experience, and we might even preserve an open mind about whether it was actually experience *of* these things; but we would not simply accept their existence until it was conclusively disproved, however long a history the belief had behind it, and however respectable and high-minded the believers. Doubt would be the only rational course.

We may first dispose of a feature common to many discussions of this kind, but which is nevertheless partly irrelevant: namely, the psychological causes and origins of religious belief. An argument common to many religious works of the past (and not a few of the present) relies on the alleged inexplicability of the more striking and mystical religious experiences, which can only be removed by invoking the supernatural. The question ' Whence come these wonderful things if not from God ? ' is fairly typical of this view. Conversely, the Freudian claim to account for the origins of belief in natural terms—briefly, by regarding God as a projection of the individual's father-image—is popularly supposed to have dealt religion a fatal wound. These views are not wholly irrelevant. The first would be important if it could be shown that it was in principle impossible to explain religious experience except by invoking real objects which caused such experience: but it seems virtually impossible to uphold such a thesis, particularly since psychological science is only in its infancy. The second is important inasmuch as it might, if true, cast considerable suspicion upon religious belief. It is reasonable to suspect the assertions of interested parties: we should suspect the assertion that ' " Sinko " removes that sinking feeling ' if made by the manufacturers of ' Sinko '. Now the thesis of certain schools of psychology is that we are all interested parties, so that we are all suspect. But even the most suspect beliefs, arising from the most psychologically disreputable motives, may still be true. To say something about the causes of a belief is not to say anything about what can logically count for or against its truth.

This point illustrates a dilemma which often seems to impose itself on those who are wondering about the truth of religion. We are tempted to think that we must either accept the psychological reputability and logical truth of some one religion in its traditional and orthodox form, or else regard religion in general as little more than superstition. Thus, in this instance, we seem to be forced into a position either of accepting at least a large part of (say) traditional Christian beliefs about God and Christ as true, or of writing off Christianity as fundamentally irrational and superstitious. If we do the first, we have to regard Freud as an arch-enemy : if the second, as a mighty demythologizer. This is chiefly because those who wish to defend religion usually want to defend a particular religion, or even a particular sect. It does not seem to occur to us that the cynic's assertion that ' man makes God in his own image ' may be true, and yet at the same time religious belief may not be wholly superstitious. It may be, for instance, that there is a God, with certain definite qualities, but that we know very little about him, and tend for the most part to foist on him those qualities which we would like him to have. Indeed, religious believers would presumably hold just this view : for the adherent of any one particular creed would have to admit that the adherents of other creeds were correct in believing in God, but were ignorant of his true nature and functions; and this could be explained by our general tendency to view God anthropomorphically. Yet however widespread and deep-rooted this tendency, it would prove nothing about whether he really existed or what his qualities really were. Plainly it needs a good deal of moral and intellectual courage to admit to such profound ignorance and such enormous obstacles ; but again, this is precisely the virtue which we would expect to have to use in an enquiry of this kind.

Whether religious experience is 'hallucinatory' or 'subjective,' therefore, is not a question that can be settled by psychology. We use such terms in reference to experience only when such experience is not experience *of* something, or of the thing it is assumed to be. Thus, I may think I am seeing a bear, whereas in fact I am seeing nothing, because there is nothing there at all : I have an experience, but it is not an experience of anything. Alternatively, I may think I am seeing a bear, whereas in fact I am seeing a bush, because there is a bush but no bear : and here I am having an experience, but it is not experience of what I think it is. Both these would count as hallucinations. Most of our hallucinations, or 'subjective' experiences, are experiences which we take to be experiences of things which do, in fact, exist—quite apart from whether we have hallucinations about them or not. Bushes and bears and oases and so on do actually exist. If our religious experience is hallucinatory or subjective, however, it must be so in rather a different sense. For on this view, there is nothing that could be the object of religious experience, in the way that there are things which could be the object of sense-experience. In a restricted sense of ' hallucination ' we cannot have a hallucination about God if there is no God, any more than we could have hallucinations about bears if there were not such things as bears.

Thus the view which we have to meet is not that certain religious experiences are illusory, for that might be taken to imply that there are other such experiences which are not illusory. It is rather that the whole of religious experience is illusory, in the sense that, if we take it to refer to real objects, we deceive ourselves, and it is this large-scale, radical attack which turns the problem into a philosophical one. For if we want to know whether a particular experience in the natural world—say, a vision of a dagger—is illusory or not, we have no need of the philosopher : we simply check up by other experiences—trying to touch and feel what we think we see, for instance. There are such things as daggers, and we know what sort of experience-tests a thing must pass if we are to believe it to be one. But if somebody were to tell us, for example, that the whole of our sense-experience was illusory, then we should feel rather more baffled and uncomfortable : we should wonder what sort of reasons could be advanced for such a view, and might call in the philosopher to help us.

Suppose we take this charge seriously for a moment. Some philosophers have a short way of dealing with it, as follows :— ' If you deny that physical objects are real,' they would say, ' and say that all our sense-experience is illusory, then you rob the words " real " and " illusory " of all their meaning. You can only talk sensibly about " illusions ", " subjective experience ", " myths " and so on if there is at least the possibility of contrasting these with what is not illusory and what is objectively real, just as you can only talk sensibly about dreams in contrast to waking life, and about counterfeit coins if there is a genuine currency for them to imitate. Physical objects, on the contrary, act as models for our application of words like " real " and " objective "; and sense-experience is at least the archetype, if not the only type, of genuine, non-illusory experience. If the physical world is not real, then nothing is ; so that to say that it is unreal is not to say anything. It would make no practical difference whether we accepted your statement or not.'

All this is quite true, but it masks an important point. It is indeed silly to ask whether the whole of our sense-experience is illusory, or whether physical objects really exist. But one of the things which someone, who feels inclined to ask such a question, wants to know is this : How much of the external world, real though it undoubtedly is, do we construct for ourselves, and how much is given to us? How much do we invent, and how much is (as it were) handed to us on a plate? How much do we write the world for ourselves, and how much do we simply read it off? These are vague questions, but meaningful ones. Thus, it is a fact that the new-born child does not immediately awaken into a perception of tables, trees, people and all the other furniture of the physical world which we, as adults, are inclined to regard as immovable fittings—as irrevocably ' given ', ' real ' and ' objective '. In the same way, a man born blind who recovers his eyesight late in life has to learn to use his eyes. From these and other facts we can induce that we do actually construct a good deal, at least, of what we later come to consider as real and ' given '. We build our worlds up for ourselves : and the fact that we usually build up worlds which are approximately similar, so that we can communicate with each other, is simply a contingent fact, and not a logical necessity.

It thus appears that even our most straightforward assertions are to some extent based on our early world-building. How do we know that the thing in the next room is a zebra? Because we can have such-and-such experiences from it : because it passes such-and-such verification-tests. But how do we know these tests are the right ones ? Because what we mean by ' zebra ' is something that passes these tests. That is the smooth, slick philosophical answer to the sceptic. But he may proceed : why should we swallow all this ? Why should we group these verification-tests round some ' object ', when the only reason we have for believing that it is an object is that it passes the tests? Perhaps we can hardly help doing so, since we do in fact have common experiences of perception, which are recurrent, and seem to fall naturally into groups ; and hence we naturally believe in the existence of permanent objects which give rise to the recurrent perceptions. But this answer hardly seems very cogent. It may be natural to act as we do : but is it necessary?

Of course it is not logically necessary : it is only practically advantageous. Consider noises. The human ear compasses and reacts to only a certain range of frequencies. We can hear the lowest note of the double-bass, and the highest note of the piccolo. Frequencies beyond our auditory range are not noises : they are subsonic or supersonic. Now noises are (apart from noises in our ears) certainly real. But suppose that, owing to the influence of cosmic rays or some equally mysterious cause, our range suddenly changed, and became higher ; so that we could all hear the squeak of bats and even supersonic frequencies, and the double-bass became totally inaudible to anyone with normal hearing. The double-bass would then no longer be making a noise : for an inaudible noise is a contradiction. Here, then, is a case where the external world would not have changed at all : only our ears would have changed. Yet what we regarded as ' a real noise ' *would* have changed, and if anyone with normal hearing said that he heard a double-bass or a low note on the organ, we should call it a hallucination. Plainly, therefore, we list things in the external world to suit our own convenience ; for unless we are scientists, we are uninterested in noises that we cannot hear : so uninterested that we should not call them noises.

Fortunately, however, the range of our senses does not change in the rather upsetting manner described above ; and, further, nearly all of us share the same range. So much do we have in common, indeed, that we can describe the world in the same terms, and use the same tests for our assertions. For by the time that we have spent a few years in the world, we have all of us come to share much the same view of it : so that it seems incredible to us that it could ever be considered otherwise. Yet it is logically possible ; and to a being equipped with different sense-organs, it would be empirically possible also. Imagine a person with an entirely different range of colour-vision, a different auditory range, a different sense of smell, and so forth. The world would look entirely different to him. He would be able to have experiences which we could not, and vice versa. Which of the two worlds is the real one, ours or his? Plainly the question is without meaning : we could equally well answer ' neither ' or ' both '. One is advantageous for us, the other for him. It is a matter of practical convenience only.

Briefly, then, our assumptions about the reality of the world and its furniture are based on (a) our common and recurrent experiences, and (b) the fact that we find it useful to group them in certain ways. There is nothing particularly disappointing about this conclusion, indeed, it is surely to be expected. Ultimately we have only two basic kinds of resources in this world : our experiences, and our desires or purposes. To hope for some sort of magical assurance about the ' ultimate reality ' of physical objects, apart from the ordinary assurance of our experience, is to hope for an impossibility, and once we can see that this ordinary assurance is perfectly satisfactory, we have no need to indulge in a wild-goose chase.

These points should give us some help in approaching the central problem : the problem of how, if at all, religious experience can qualify as cognitive experience. Many philosophers to-day would deny the cognitive quality of religious experience, and *ipso facto* the existence of religious ' objects ' to which the experience relates. This denial seems based, perhaps unconsciously, on two misconceptions which it may be helpful at this stage to state in a general form. They are (1) that there is a basic, ontological difference between what can be said to exist and what cannot, and (2) that only perceptions or sense-experience can be cognitive (only sense-data can really be data). These views are not analytically true, and they are not empirical certainties ; but they form a creed which is implicit in much of the philosophy of the past few decades. To elucidate and criticize these two views in turn may help to clarify the problem.

(1) We can distinguish three types of talk :

(a) Talk about private experiences, as when I say ' I feel pain ', or ' I hear a buzzing in my ears '. These are private experiences ; for though it is possible for other people to have similar experiences, they cannot have the same or the identical experiences, just because they are not myself. Other people can have buzzings in their ears, but they cannot have my buzzing.

(b) Talk about public experiences : for instance, the experiences people have when seeing and touching a penny, or listening to Brahms.

(c) Talk about objects or things, like a penny, or a symphony.

Now what are the differences between these types of talk? It is sometimes said that the first two are only talk about experiences, and have no reference to ' the outside world ', whereas the third is talk about what ' really exists '. But this is very misleading, and suggests that the first two somehow fall short in giving useful or reliable information. Yet to say ' Wilson feels pain ' or ' Everyone in the concert-hall felt over-

whelmed by what they heard ' may be very useful: and to
somebody who is not Wilson and who was not in the concert-
hall, these statements would certainly give information about
' the outside world '. The experiences of Wilson and the
audience certainly ' really exist ': they are part of the world
just as much as tables and chairs. In other words, this talk is
not somehow bogus or deceptive: it is not about something
which has a kind of pseudo-existence.

The difference is better expressed in terms of general and
permanent utility. Talk about an individual's private experiences is genuinely informative, but its usefulness for the public
is strictly limited. Like most autobiography, one cannot
usefully generalize from it: the fact that I have a buzzing in
my ears can only have, as it were, a second-hand interest to
others. Again, to record publicly-shared experiences does not
in itself enable the public to arrange their lives any more con-
veniently for the future, for instance by enabling them to
anticipate further experiences under similar conditions. To
say that everyone in the concert-hall felt overwhelmed by
what they heard on such-and-such an evening is not to say
anything permanently reliable about Brahms. But if we
commit ourselves to the third type of talk—' existential ' talk,
if we like to call it so—we thereby commit ourselves to a
generalization from experience: we say that certain experiences are available to any observer whatsoever who fulfills
certain specifiable conditions.

This accounts for the logical fact that one cannot *translate*
an existential statement by any number of statements about
experiences, however large: not even if these latter include
references to future or potential experiences. ' There is a
penny on the table ' does not *mean* ' Such-and-such sense-
experiences are always available to anybody with normal
senses under such-and-such conditions ', however carefully or
fully we specify the experiences and the conditions. The price
we pay for making these existential generalizations is that (as
with all other generalizations) we may be mistaken in certain
instances. But this logical difference between the two kinds of
talk is not the whole story; it does not point to a basic difference

in reality. Existential statements are a kind of convenient shorthand, which could often—so far as practical purposes go—be written out fully in experience-statements, even though these would not be an exact translation. Thus, it would be possible to specify a certain number of available experiences—that one could feel so-and-so, see such-and-such, and so on—instead of saying simply ' There is a penny ': and this speci-fication would be good enough for practical purposes. A child who wanted to buy a gob-stopper would be content with believing that he could pick up what seemed to be some-thing hard and flat and round, take it to a shop, and receive in exchange something which appeared to be, and tasted like, a gob-stopper. Logically, something may always occur to upset an existential statement like ' There is a penny '; but in practice, it may be so well supported by true statements about experience that we should be justified in saying that such a contingency was impossible. There is a difference between logical entailment and common-sense implication : we may say that logically no number of experience-statements entails an existential statement, but that in practice a sufficient number may be taken to imply it.

Since many of our experiences are common and recurrent, we find the existential shorthand very convenient. ' Object-ivity ' and ' existence ' are not basic features of reality, but titles whereby we dignify sets of common and recurrent experi-ences which do not let us down. In our bestowing of these titles, we are not recognizing but rather, in a sense, deciding ; our decisions are based on the reasonable grounds of practical convenience, and it would be very hard to avoid making them. What we assert, for practical purposes, is the same sort of thing as we assert in experience-statements. This we can see from considering the tests for both sorts of statements. ' There is a penny ' and its practical equivalent in experience-statements would, in fact, both have to pass the same tests. The tests would be logically conclusive for the experience-statements, and only practically conclusive for the existential : but that is the only significant difference.

What we have to consider, therefore, is simply whether any

existential statements which we might make in a religious or any other context would be useful and reliable : whether we are justified in making the decisive jump from experience-statements to existential ones, or whether the former would be equally convenient. For instance, suppose that we are wondering whether it is correct to say ' I feel a pain ' or ' There exists a pain within me ', we should not decide this question by an ontological enquiry about whether pain is a thing which really exists or not. It is largely a matter of taste whether we choose to call pain a thing which exists. We should rather point out that nothing is gained by saying ' There exists a pain ', and that the verification of this is no more extensive than of ' I feel a pain ', and that therefore ' There exists a pain ' does not help anybody with any more information than its non-existential counterpart. These are practical considerations rather than logical or ontological ones.

An apparently existential statement such as ' There is a God ', therefore, would have to imply that certain experiences are generally and permanently available, at least to certain people under certain conditions, just as ' grass is green ' implies that certain people (those who are not blind or colour-blind) under certain conditions (in a normal light, and without the use of rose-tinted spectacles) would have common experiences for which we use the word ' green '. It would not have to imply that a *majority* of people would have these experiences, or that there were sophisticated scientific tests which could replace them. We should (and did) correctly believe in the existence of colours without either knowing that the majority of people were not colour-blind, or being able to measure light-waves given off by colours. All we need is a certain number of people with a common and recurrent experience, and some way of distinguishing genuine from illusive experience. Just as we can say ' I seemed to see something green, but I was wrong ', so we must be able to say ' I seemed to experience God, but I was wrong'. And provided ' There is a God ' asserts the permanent possibility of a varied number of experiences, it is always possible for us to be deceived, and hence by further experience-tests to realize that we have been

deceived. We could say, perhaps, ' Experiences *a*, *b* and *c*
made me think I was in touch with God : but experiences *d*,
e and *f*, which I also had, made me change my mind.' This
would be like saying ' Certain experiences made me think it
was a man, but others made me change my mind and think it
was a waxwork.'

(2) The view that only sense-experience can be cognitive
seems either to be mere dogma, or to rest on a misunderstanding. When we are born, we have certain experiences
which we afterwards categorize under the two headings of
' perceptions ' and ' feelings '. But this categorization is made
for practical purposes. We find that some experiences are
recurrent under certain conditions, and common to others as
well as ourselves. Most (but in my view, not all) of these are
perceptions, and we come to use perception-words like ' see ',
' hear ', ' touch ', and the word ' perceive ' itself transitively,
in reference to the external objects which for the sake of convenience we have constructed from our own experience and
the guidance of others. Most (but again, perhaps not all) of
what we come to call ' feelings ' do not recur commonly ; so
that there is no point in our regarding them as cognitive, or in
believing in objects from which they derive. Since most of us
have the same sense-organs, and since these organs function
similarly in almost everyone, we are all in general agreement
about what is cognitive experience and what is not : and
similarly about what exists and what does not. But this is, so
to speak, a mere biological accident : it is not a logical
limitation. There may be—certainly, there logically can be—
cognitive ' feelings ' : or, if we prefer to express it otherwise,
some of what we now call ' feelings ' may be ' perceptions '.
Amongst these may be, for instance, the appreciation of human
personality, of works of art, and of the supernatural.

So much for the dogma. The misunderstanding is this.
Suppose we assert that in appreciating music our feelings are
cognitive—that we really experience the beauty or majesty or
whatever in the music, and can make useful existential
assertions about the qualities of the music. Someone may say
' Ah, but all you *really* experience is the actual sounds made

by the instruments : the rest is only in your own mind.' This is a good instance of the way in which ' real ' tends to be equated with ' concrete' or ' material'. But we might equally well say of seeing a penny ' Ah, all we *really* see is an elliptic brown patch : the rest is just in our own minds.' In an obvious sense this could be true ; but it would be like saying of a man telephoning a friend ' Ah, he's not *really* talking to Smith, he's just talking to the telephone ' or of a man driving a car ' Ah, he's not *really* turning the wheels, he's just turning the steering-wheel.' In these last three cases these remarks are obviously misconceived. How do we know whether or not such a remark would be misconceived in the first case? Not by considering the physical quality of the experience itself, and disqualifying it if it were not the hardest possible kind of sense-experience. We should enquire whether there were good grounds for making existential assertions about music : whether there was a testing-system for such assertions : and whether such assertions were publicly useful, in the general and permanent way that we require. The temptation to regard as genuine only that experience which looks scientifically respectable must be resisted : and a programme designed to remove from the world all that human beings write into it would end, not in a pure and uncontaminated residue of objective reality, but in sheer vacancy.

If we do not allow these two views to mislead us, therefore, it is possible to see how both religious and other experience might qualify for the title of ' cognitive '. Remembering our analogy with roulette-playing in the last section, we shall not be unduly disturbed by the fact that religious words like ' God ' may have different meanings for different religious groups, or that different groups may have different verification-systems for their assertions. We shall also sympathetically take into account one probability : namely, that the conditions for obtaining genuine religious experience may be very stringent. Everyone has some sense of touch, and everyone who is not blind can see things : but it may be that not everyone can experience the supernatural. Alternatively—a more encouraging outlook—it may be that many people, at least in certain societies, have to learn how to have this experience, just as we all learn as children how to use our physical senses. Or perhaps, again, we all once knew how to have it, but the knowledge has been repressed in us for some sociological reason or other. Any of these obstacles would make it difficult for religion to establish a large number of true assertions : but the difficulty would be practical, not logical.

D. *Testing Religious Assertions*

So far we have followed the rather negative programme of asserting the logical possibility of informative religious assertions, and trying to show that they are not disqualified *a priori* from meeting the requirements which they are supposed to meet. We are now bound to describe, at least in a general form, how a testing-system for these assertions, based on religious experience, could be made to work ; and it must at once be admitted that the difficulties are considerable. However, since I hope to have shown that they are practical rather than logical difficulties, they should not be insuperable. It is important to remember that in dealing with the physical world, we have the advantage of five senses which work in conjunction with each other : so that we can always think of a large number of tests for empirical assertions, relying on a system of cross-checking between one sense and another. Thus, if we are not sure whether we really see what we seem to see, we can go up to it and try to touch it, or smell it, or taste it. We must not expect to be so favoured in non-natural fields of experience.

It has often been observed that there is a close parallel between aesthetic talk and religious talk, and between the types of experience which prompt such talk. Just as religious talk is (in one sense) meaningless to the non-believer, so talk about music, for instance, seems meaningless to the tone-deaf; and just as we doubt whether religious experience is ' objective ' or ' cognitive ', so we doubt whether the qualities which music-lovers claim to be in various compositions are ' really there ', or exist merely in their own minds. Again, the two facts (a) that we have no sophisticated or scientific tests to assess the merits of music, and (b) that probably only a small minority of people appreciate the great classical composers, are paralleled in the field of religion. Finally, the process of learning how to appreciate music might be considered as basically similar to the process of learning how to experience God or to have some similar religious experience.

Yet if we are free of some of the philosophical prejudices which I have been criticizing in the last section, it is not difficult to see that there does exist a testing-system for assertions about musical merit. We all know, in fact, the optimum conditions for testing of this kind : it involves a complete lack of prejudice, a certain amount of factual knowledge about musical form, a wide experience of all kinds of music, and constant experience of the work being assessed, repeated over a long period of time. These tests are not completely watertight—no testing-system is—but they are sufficiently conclusive for us to have reached a considerable measure of agreement about the qualities of many works and many composers. We accept, even if not unreservedly, the judgement of music critics : that is, of people who are in a better position than ourselves to make the tests. We hold classes in musical appreciation, on the assumption that we are here dealing with real qualities about which we can make existential assertions.

If someone wants to judge a piece of music correctly, he knows quite well what to do. He clears his mind of other matters, listens to it carefully over a period of time, and then forms his opinion on the basis of his feelings or perceptions. If he is uncertain, he may say simply ' I like that ', or ' That gives me a thrill ', or ' That seems to me good, but I'm not sure if it really is '. If he becomes certain, he begins to make more definite statements : ' Brahms's first symphony is immensely powerful ', ' Mozart's last three piano concertos are tragic, not merely pretty ', ' The recitative in Bach's St. Matthew Passion is often poignant ', and so forth. These statements are comprehensible at least within the large group of music-lovers who have the experiences to which words like ' powerful ', ' tragic ', ' poignant ', ' romantic ', and so forth, refer; for, of course, these words have specialized or technical meanings, often ill-defined, but quite recognizable to anyone who has had the experiences which they are used to express. Hence a circle of musicians can carry on an interesting and wholly genuine argument in language which seems either misleading or nonsensical to someone outside the circle.

Statements of this kind are certainly not about the private experience of the person who makes them. Nor, in point of strict logic, can they be completely translated into statements about the public experiences of a wider selection of people. Hence it is possible to say, first, ' This seems majestic to me, but I know it isn't ', and secondly, ' Most people find that Offenbach appeals to them more than Bach, but in fact Bach is much better '. The statements we are considering are perfectly genuine assertions, on a par with existential assertions about material objects and qualities. They are generalizations from experience, of course, just as statements about material objects are; but some of them at least are so well-founded, and based on such reliable experience, that we use the short-hand, existential form of speech, and assume—or decide— that we are talking about qualities actually to be found in the music, not merely about our own experiences. The weakness of saying something like ' Most people find that Offenbach appeals to them more than Bach, but in fact Bach is much better ' is not a logical weakness, for ' Bach is much better ' is not intended to be verifiable by the experience of a majority, nor by scientific tests: in the way that ' Most people cannot hear bats squeak, but in fact bats do squeak ' might be scientifically verifiable. The testing-system is not based on the immediate and untrained reactions of a majority, but on what experiences are obtained by those willing to put themselves in a position to receive them. Such a position is reached, not by a long course of indoctrination in favour of or against certain types of music, but simply by learning to open one's mind more fully to what one hears.

Assertions about musical merit, then, like ordinary empirical assertions, are to the effect that under certain conditions (when one is appreciating music properly) certain people (those who are not tone-deaf) will have certain experiences. It is plainly possible to make false assertions under this testing-system, and these can be decisively falsified by the system, if the experiences do not occur. In a sense, any true assertion will have predictive value; as anyone who is trying to appreciate and enjoy music knows, a reliable assertion is very useful. If I want to be moved, and accept some critic's assertion that Wagner is very moving, and also discover this to be true, I shall be right in saying that he has made a true and useful prediction; and it is on predictions of this kind—predictions inherent in the assertions themselves—that knowledge about musical merit is based. All this is obviously parallel to empirical assertions, and the predictions inherent in them which point to future or potential experiences.

Of course we can—many people do—refuse to accept all this. It may seem to us rather like making assertions about what will happen if we take some drug which affects our sense-experience, like mescalin. No doubt anyone who takes mescalin will experience certain things, and no doubt we can regard these things as ' really existing ' if we like, and no doubt we can build up a testing-system for verifying and falsifying assertions about them. But there seems no point in doing so. Naturally there is no point, for our experiences under the influence of mescalin do not form part of our normal life. They are of no use to us, and we have no motive for combining them into an objective framework. In the case of our normal sense-experience, we have the strongest possible motive, as we have already seen in the last section: but mescalin experiences would be of interest to us only as a psychological oddity. This is not true of musical appreciation. Logically, one could dismiss our experiences of music as mere oddities, and of no interest to our daily lives; but we should be throwing away so much that many people found worth while that it would be unreasonable to do so.

The case for using—or if necessary constructing—a testing-system for religious assertions, therefore, rests upon two assumptions: (a) that under certain conditions certain people would always have certain experiences, such that reliable

existential assertions could be made to incorporate them, and
(b) that these experiences would be of sufficient interest and
importance to us to make it worth our while to do this. Of
course this is a minimum case. In fact religion could claim
much more than this. It might claim, for instance, that a vast
majority of people could be taught to have the experiences,
and that the experiences were so striking and important that
we should give priority to any programme concerned with
clarifying and expressing them. This claim I believe to be
true; but it would only be found to be true by first using the
testing-system. Perhaps this is a rather arid way of saying
what believers say, when they insist that the first step is to
learn how to experience God.

We must imagine, then, a programme designed to permit as
many people as possible to have religious experience. It is
hard to say just what form this would take: this is a matter
for religious experts, and not for philosophers. We could guess,
however, that it would involve freeing the mind from the dis-
tractions of the senses, and training it to try to experience
something general beneath the myriad particulars of the world.
Religious experience is unlike aesthetic appreciation, of course,
in that one is not presented with something definite, like a
symphony or a painting, towards which one can direct one's
whole attention, but it is plain, nevertheless, that certain
symbols or certain situations may help. The mental attitudes
appropriate to specifically religious situations, such as prayer,
or worship, or repentance, may yield the kind of fruit we
require, or it may be possible to disentangle from the mystics
something sufficiently manageable for our requirements. The
programme may take some time, and those who undertake it
may need (as with aesthetic appreciation) to be sympathetically inclined towards the possibility of experience, whilst
reserving their intellectual judgement. But there is no reason
why it should not give us the results we need.

I need hardly say that such a programme must be carried
through without bias. If, whenever the tests yield negative
results, we simply tell the subject that he has not tried hard
enough, we shall obviously be cheating: a form of dishonesty

which I am bound to say seems to be in constant use amongst
religious groups. We must remember that we are open in
principle and in logic to decisive falsification as well as verification, even though evidence that is actually decisive may be
lacking : otherwise we shall never reach a position in which
we can make an informative assertion. Yet we must also
remember that the experience may, indeed, be difficult to
attain, and that this need throw no doubt upon its genuineness.
Again, our analogy with music affords some help. It is
legitimate to tell people who do not appreciate Bach that they
are not trying hard enough, or not giving the music a fair
chance : but there comes a point where such injunctions
would look suspicious, if there did not already exist a large
group of people whose experience of Bach was significantly
reliable. We need above all to establish such a group in
religion : and we may find that more than one such group
actually exists.

The way in which we might come to make assertions might
be something like this : The subjects of our programme might
come to have certain common experiences which always
recurred under certain conditions. Call these experiences
' love ', ' grace ', ' power ', ' majesty ', ' beauty ', and so on,
remembering that these are technical terms. Then we construct, recognize, or decide to acknowledge an entity from
which these experiences flow. We call this entity God. Then
we can say, for instance, ' God is love.' This implies that
whenever we have enough experiences for us to be able to say
that we are confronting God, we should always have a simul-
taneous experience of love. Such an implication makes the
assertion ' God is love ' decisively falsifiable. Again, we may
have experiences which strongly resemble the experience of
meeting a person. In certain contexts we may find these
associated with other experiences : first, with love, grace,
friendship, help, and so on, so that we may wish to talk about
' meeting God ', or with hatred, horror, ugliness, etc., so that
we may wish to talk about ' encountering the Devil'. These
too would be decisively falsifiable statements. We should be
able to say ' I thought I was meeting God, but I wasn't ', or

' It seems to me that Christ is present with me, but I'm not sure '. Further tests in terms of the experiences which form the criteria for the application of words like ' God ' might make us more sure, or alternatively convince us that we were wrong. All this is logically parallel to empirical talk and tests.

Such a programme is bound to appear naive and vague ; but the chief reason for this is that there is no common language whereby we can refer precisely to certain experiences. Different religious groups have different terminologies, which may have more or less precise usages within the groups ; but since the common testing-system does not yet exist, the usage is bound to seem vague to the non-believer. For instance, an assertion like ' Christ answers prayer ' seems impossibly difficult to verify, unless one happens to be a member of a sect for which it has a precise meaning. Yet one can see how we might be able to reach agreement about giving it a precise meaning which would be acceptable to everybody, if only for the purposes of further investigation and testing. Similarly ' God ' plainly means quite different things to different religious groups : but we might agree to adopt basic and minimal criteria for its universal application.

What we have outlined, however, is a kind of minimum programme designed to give an agreed meaning to religious terms like ' God ', which may result in agreement about the objective existence of God and other supernatural entities. This programme, so far as it goes, suits the empirical world of objects and sense-experience, the world of aesthetics, and the world of the supernatural ; in the sense that it outlines the minimal conditions for meaning, verification and objective existence, it does equal justice to all three. But in other ways it is plain that the three realms differ. God is not an object, nor an aesthetic quality, and it is important to realize some of the logical differences here, for a programme which could only lead us to a God who was logically like a table or like the majesty of a Beethoven symphony would hardly be of much help to religion. Nobody worships tables or symphonies.

It is plain where the aesthetic analogy breaks down. Both physical objects and people interact with us in a way that aesthetic qualities do not. All three can, in their separate ways, affect us. Objects can hit us, people can like us, aesthetic qualities can stir our feelings. But the converse is not true. We can *do* things to objects and to people : but we cannot do things to aesthetic qualities—we can only adopt certain attitudes towards them. Moreover, it is possible to adopt an attitude of complete neutrality towards works of art : we do not *have* to look at them or experience them ; whereas we cannot avoid engagement with the world of objects, nor—unless we live on a desert island—with the world of people. We might say that aesthetic qualities are there only to be experienced if we wish : it is a real world, but a world which we cannot touch : we can only lay ourselves open to it. Our relationship with it is not a two-way process.

Belief in the God of any religion, however, definitely requires a two-way process. God is supposed to be real in a manner analogous to that in which a person is real, someone who acts and is acted upon. In other words, our programme has to be capable not merely of building up an entity but of building up a particular kind of entity, a person-like entity. The entity must be like an object insofar as our relationship with it is a two-way process ; but it must also be more than that. It must be like a person, insofar as our relationship with it must be personal. Any God with whom such a relationship was impossible would hardly be a God of religion : he might be the remote and disengaged supervisor of an ethic or a way of life, but the personal feelings of awe and worship would be to some extent inappropriate. The ' I-Thou ' relationship would be lacking : for one of the things that distinguishes people from physical objects is that the former act upon us in a way similar to the way in which we act upon them. They are people, because they behave like us. Thus God is supposed to be aware of the thoughts and behaviour of all men, whether or not they choose to believe in or enter upon the supernatural realm, in a way that physical objects or aesthetic qualities are not aware.

Yet there is no reason why our programme, which is merely a logical skeleton for the establishment of *any* kind of entity, should not prove capable of showing the reality of such a being. We can hardly expect any very plausible analogies here, since we are now concerned with the kind of entity to be established and not with what is logically common to all entities. But there are some things in which we believe that seem like half-way houses on the road to belief in a person. We might, for instance, believe (like Wordsworth) in a Spirit behind nature, or (like the ancient Greeks and Romans) in Love. To give these words capital letters is not simply a piece of poetic whimsy : it points to the fact that those who believe in such things regard them almost as people. It is at least *as if* the Spirit of Nature of the Spirit of Love acted upon them and made them behave in certain ways : as if they were aware of human beings, and had a life of their own, irrespective of whether human beings believed in them or not. They surround us and call to us as people call : to disregard them is not merely to miss something but to behave unrealistically, to pretend that the powers do not exist when they are only too real. All this is not too remote from belief in a personal God.

Just as we know what to expect from objects by way of experience, so we know what to expect from people : and just as we can collect experiences of touch and taste and vision, so we can collect experiences of being loved, being answered, being comforted and being directed. If there is a personal God, then we must be able to have experiences of a person : just those experiences, in fact, which religious believers claim to have. Like any other experiences, these can be false or veridical, fragmentary or recurrent, sufficient to justify the language of existence or insufficient. We cannot decide this *a priori*, though as things stand each individual may have to make an intelligent guess one way or the other. We shall only reach a permanently satisfactory settlement by carrying through the programme of investigation.

E. Some other features of Religious Language

To conclude this chapter, I should like to investigate certain points which may be of use to the would-be believer, if he accepts the theoretical and practical possibility of religious truth and knowledge along the lines we have indicated. Our concern with those religious assertions which are supposed to contain information about the supernatural, and on which anything that could properly be called a religion must primarily rely, should nevertheless not blind us to the problems and confusions inherent in the rest of religious language. Particularly if we are assessing a specific religion, creed, or sect, and trying to descover the way in which it works logically, it is important that we should appreciate something of the variety and characteristics of religious language as a whole.

1. *Variety*

It is impossible to determine accurately how any particular assertion or group of words is used in the language of a religion, without being thoroughly familiar with the context of the religion as a whole and the way in which the assertion is brought into that context. I should suspect that only a philosopher who was, so to speak, on the inside of a religion could feel any real confidence in analysing its terms successfully. It is open to anyone, however, to point to different usages that might exist within various religions; and there is little doubt that many believers would have no hesitation in accepting that these usages did exist. Without being determined to pin different usages specifically on to different individual assertions, therefore, we may nevertheless give a brief and general account of the variety of usage itself.

Some of this variety we have already noticed *en passant*. In the previous chapter we made a simple and straightforward— perhaps a rather naive—distinction between four types of religious talk: between assertions of value or morality, assertions of historical or empirical fact, assertions designed to clarify how religious terms are used in their context, and assertions which appeared to assert supernatural facts. Even these four simple categories, however, are not always readily to be distinguished from each other in religious language. The Athanasian Creed of Christianity, for instance, might seem to be a series of factually informative statements, telling us what God and the Trinity are like, and professedly based on the experience of believers. But it might also fulfil other functions. It might be, as it were, laying down logical and linguistic rules for talk about God and the Trinity: establishing words in the framework of Christian terminology, rather than establishing facts about the objects of Christian belief: recording Christian decisions about appropriate language, rather than recording Christian discoveries about the nature of the divine. There is no doubt that a great deal of theology is of this kind.

Again, we are often prone to muddle up historical and supernatural information. Strictly speaking, a statement like ' It is a historical fact that the Son of God was born amongst men ', is simply untrue. History does not deal with the supernatural: we have already seen that it is misleading to bring in the divine as part of a historical or scientific explanation. ' It is a historical fact that a man called Jesus was born amongst men ' is an unexceptionable statement: but the temptation to smuggle in our religious beliefs in the phrase ' The Son of God ' should be resisted for the sake of clarity. Assertions involving value or morality, also, can be easily confused with assertions about the supernatural. According to many believers, ' good ' can always be taken as equivalent to ' the will of God ', for instance. Yet the first word is a term of value, and the second phrase, together with other phrases like ' what Christ wants me to do ', and so on, is simply a description of supernatural fact. It may appear pedantic to criticize confusions of this kind, and doubtless it would present no difficulty to clear them up: but at the present time, when the investigation of religious belief demands clarity above all else, I do not think that we can afford to speak loosely. ' Good ' does not *mean* ' the will of God ', even though what is good may always in practice coincide with what is God's will for us. To remember this, together with the fact that different people think different things good whereas God's will is presumably unchanging, might perhaps make us somewhat hesitant in professing to know God's will, and hence lessen the danger, always notorious in religion, of believers bringing in God to support their own possibly ignoble desires.

We also noticed some other functions which certain religious language may have. The view that what look like genuinely informative assertions may really be myths or stories designed to support the believer's way of life is undoubtedly true to an extent: that is, there exist religions which would persuade their adherents to believe these stories not on the grounds that they are in actual fact true, but on the grounds that they are morally helpful and that they increase faith. Again, much religious language can be described as ' ritualistic ' ; and this is correct, inasmuch as believers do use it, and admit to using it, in this way. There are other functions, however, which are rarely noticed by non-believers, and not always consciously appreciated by believers. Several thinkers have correctly stressed the difference between talking *about* God, and talking *to* God. This is perhaps a bigger difference than any we have noticed so far. We have noticed that we can talk about many different things: about the supernatural, about historical fact, about values, or about the words and logic of our own discourse. But much—possibly most—of the language actually used by believers is in some sense talk to the supernatural, or talk designed to bring them in touch with the supernatural. The language used by believers when praying, confessing, worshipping, repenting, exhorting or praising is not supposed to be informative language at all. It fulfils other psychological purposes, which it is inadequate to dismiss as ' poetic ' or ' emotional ' or ' persuasive '. Some of it, as in confession, is designed to put the believer into a state of mind whereby he can realize his own position in relation to God ; some of it, as in repentance, makes him able to accept the power of God within himself; some of it, as in worship and praise, endeavours to lift him up to God.

These latter functions concern the believer rather than the philosopher ; and once the philosopher has given some help in analysing them, there is little more that he can do. But he can be of more use in considering the informative assertions, by pointing out the methods of verification on which they may rely. Thus, if a believer asks why he should believe this or that assertion, the answer given by his church may be :

   (i) Because it is capable of proof by his experience.
  (ii) Because it is analytically true, or true by definition or deduction.
 (iii) Because a certain authority says so.
 (iv) Because it is a historical fact.

These are only some of the answers that may be given, though they are perhaps the most common. It is obviously important for the believer to be able to distinguish between these various types of answers, so that he may see how the structure of his faith has been erected : and it is even more important for the would-be believer to do so, in order that he may assess the merits and demerits of that structure. It might even be possible to classify religions according to the logic of their structure, calling some ' religions of personal experience ', others ' religions of authority ', and so on.

If the structure is to stand up at all, of course, it must contain at least some informative assertions of type (i) : i.e. assertions demonstrable by experience. It is often difficult, however, to distinguish these from type (ii), the analytic assertions ; and to both of these most religions add many assertions of type (iii) based on some authority, and not a few of type (iv), assertions of historical fact. We must appreciate that each of these has its own peculiar weaknesses. Statements of type (i) have to stand the test of experience, and are in consequence not only vulnerable, but vulnerable in proportion to their informativeness ; (ii) achieve invulnerability only by failing to inform us about facts : they are useful as a guide to the logic and language of our beliefs, but they give us no foundation for them in the outside world ; (iii) are only useful provided the authority is trustworthy : in the eyes of a radical critic they merely push his questions back a stage or two ; (iv) are again vulnerable in just the same way as they are informative : if we found a religion on history, we must be prepared to abandon it if the historical facts turn out to be different from what we had thought. When we consider certain specific beliefs, it is easy to see both that it is not always clear which method of verification we are supposed to use, and that it is impossible to assess the truth of the beliefs unless we clear up

this point first. For instance, is the Christian belief in the
Virgin Birth of Christ supposed to rest on the acceptance of a
religious authority, or on plain history? Does one believe it
because the Church or the Bible says so, or because it is a
historical fact? Again, does the doctrine of the Trinity rest
upon rules of Christian language, existing merely as a
deduction from other statements, or is it capable of proof by
experience, or should it simply be accepted on the authority
of a church or churches? These questions are logically prior;
and they too often pass unnoticed in debate.

2. *Expandibility*

Religious believers hold, quite correctly, that we can only
hope to know a very little about God : and most believers
would naturally object to a programme of testing, such as we
have suggested, which would tie words like ' God ' down to
our tested experiences alone. Here we seem to be in a
dilemma : if we tie them down, we narrow their meaning
unduly, and if we do not, we allow ourselves to use words
without any reference to our experience, so that they are in
danger of becoming meaningless.

But the dilemma is more apparent than real. For, in the
first place, although any informative assertion about God
must be based on experience, we can do other things with the
word ' God ' besides using it merely as a name for collective
experience. For instance, we can translate it analytically into
other terms, such as ' the Almighty Father ', ' the Spirit of
love ', or ' the Lord of the Universe ' : terms which might link
up with other experiences. Moreover, we do not have to tie
' God ' down to our own experiences : we can rest the word on
the experiences of other people past and present, and trust
their assertions about God whenever these seem reliable. In
the second place, we do not have to tie the word down in such
a way as to deny ourselves the possibility of incorporating
future experiences within the same concept. By ' God ' we can
mean ' at least so-and-so ', and still believe that there is a
great deal more for which the word could stand, if we could
have the necessary experiences. In this way, our increase of

knowledge about God throughout the ages will obviously enlarge our concept of God; and the word ' God ' itself will take on more meaning, and possibly different meaning. Quite radical changes and enlargements can happen in this way. For example, the phrase ' the earth ' or ' the world ' now means something very different from what it meant at a time when everyone thought the earth was flat, or before we knew the facts about the solar system and outer space. New experience has brought new and wider meaning.

Nor need this temporary tying-down of words to experience diminish the mystery of what we experience: though if we do not tie them down, the mystery turns into logical chaos and nonsense. The word ' Mars ' to us, as used of the planet, has a definite set of criteria for its application, derived of course from our experiences from looking through telescopes and similar methods. Yet Mars itself may still be very mysterious to us, because we know so little about it. A concept like ' space ' or ' the universe ', well-based though it may be on experience, may still remain full of mystery. We may not comprehend or be able to imagine its infinity, its wonder, its majesty, or many of its basic physical qualities. Yet we still know what we mean by ' space ': if we did not, we could not talk about space sensibly. So also with religious words. It is essential that we should know what we mean by ' God ' at any one time, and this involves basing the word firmly on experience. But this does not involve the implication that we know all about God himself.

In this way it is possible to describe many religious words and concepts as expandible or elastic. We must remember, however, that though they may be allowed to expand or stretch so as to include new meaning based on new experience, we cannot allow them to contract and shrink so as to exclude those experiences on which they are based. If these terms are to be useful for discussion, or for playing any part in informative assertions at all, there must remain a hard core of meaning which cannot be changed, though it may be enlarged. Further, we must take care that it does not become so enlarged as to approach vacuity. A pantheistic assertion about

God such as ' God is everything and everywhere ' tends to be vacuous : it is uninformative because it does not specify. A great deal of talk about God's infinity or transcendence is useful if it is intended to prevent our permanently limiting the criteria for the application of the word ' God ' : but it is dangerous if it enables us to assert anything about God that we choose to assert. For informative assertions are not arbitrary.

3. *Borrowings from empirical language*

A great deal of religious language has been drawn from empirical language. Thus, we talk about the ' love ' of God who is ' our Father ', about the ' grace ' of Christ, and so on. These are commonly described as metaphors or analogies : and the function of these metaphors and analogies has given a good deal of trouble to believers. On the one hand, we do not wish to say that they must be taken literally; but on the other hand, we wish to say that they must be taken seriously. It is not altogether easy to see how this can be managed ; and some philosophers have come to the conclusion that this sort of religious language cannot hope to be informative or useful at all, except perhaps as a means of boosting the faith and feelings of believers. But this results from a false view of the logical functions of metaphor and analogy.

Let us begin by considering metaphor. Suppose that we say that a knife is sharp, and then that a man's wits are sharp. We can say, if we like, that the first is a straightforward use of ' sharp ', and the second a metaphorical use. But this does not mean that the first use is any more exact, or meaningful, or informative, than the second. On the contrary, the criteria for the application of ' sharp ' in either case are fairly precise : only they are different criteria. They are not entirely different : it is part of the meaning of ' sharp ' in both cases that what is called ' sharp ' does its job quickly and efficiently. But in most other respects they are different. Yet ' sharp ' in the metaphorical usage is no more vague than ' sharp ' in the straightforward usage. Similarly, there is no reason why religious words like ' love ', ' grace ', and ' father ' should be vague. They are words borrowed from our everyday, natural life: applied to the supernatural, they take on different meanings, very much as words like ' force ' and ' work ' take on different meanings in the specialized field of mechanics.

The case with analogy is different. The purpose of an analogy is to clarify the way in which the words in your original statement work, what sort of logical job they are doing. The analogy makes this clear to your hearer by presenting him with the same logic in a context with which he is more familiar. Analogies clarify: naturally they do not prove anything. They are educational devices. For instance, suppose I say that there is one God, yet three Persons: one who is in heaven, one who intercedes between heaven and us, and one who cheers and comforts us on earth. All these three Persons are God, yet there is only one God. This may well baffle. Now suppose I use an ancient analogy, and say there is only one sun, yet three roles which it plays: there is the ball of burning gas in space, the rays of the sun which come from the ball of gas to earth, and the actual light and warmth of the sun on earth. Then I point out that we can use the word ' sun ' to refer to any of these: I can say either ' The sun is a long way away', or ' I am standing in the sun', or ' the sun is very warm to-day'. Of course this proves nothing about one God or three Persons: but it helps to elucidate what might be meant by talking about one God or three Persons. If the analogy is a good one, it may show that the logic of my original statement is not nonsense—that the words will do the work I set them to do. That is why analogies can do something towards conviction.

It would be quite possible for religion to do without either metaphor or analogy, and to make no borrowings from ordinary language at all. Instead of the metaphorical terms ' love ', ' grace ' and so on, with their specific religious meanings, we could invent new, technical terms to denote the experiences to which these refer, and we could do without analogies altogether. But although their retention may cause a certain amount of confusion to those who do not fully appreciate their logic, there are obvious practical reasons why it is wise to retain them. The metaphorical language creates a feeling of familiarity in the mind of the beginner : and the whole point of analogies, as we have seen, is to familiarize people, by means of well-known examples, with the logic of unfamiliar cases. They both offer a framework of understanding, even if the framework is in a sense artificial. As we know from our childhood experience, to be familiar with a word is a good start towards understanding its use.

4. *Communication with non-believers*

Finally we must briefly consider the question of how far religious language can be communicated intelligibly to, or understood by, those to whom it does not already mean something. This is, in my view, the chief problem with which religious apologetics should be concerned. For the position is not that the agnostic understands what believers say, but simply disagrees with them about the facts : it is rather that they live in different worlds—as we say, they ' speak different languages '.

We are concerned here only with the informative assertions of religion, those which assert supernatural fact : for other types of religious language present no peculiar problems. It is easy enough, for instance to give translations of religious terms : to tell the agnostic that ' God ' means ' an Almighty Father ', or that a sacrament is an outward and visible sign of an inward and spiritual grace. But this will give him no satisfaction : it may familiarize him with the terminology and the language as a whole, but it does not perform the essential function of grounding that language in reality.

It is often believed that religious assertions are incomprehensible to anyone who does not have religious experience. Strictly, this is not necessarily true. A blind man has no experience of colour, but it is incorrect to say that he does not know what words like ' red ' and ' green ' actually mean. For he can give equivalents for these words in English, and use them successfully in his conversation. He could explain to a foreigner what they meant, and understand his neighbours when they used them. In much the same way, a non-believer could successfully discover the linguistic uses of religious words; and in fact it is sufficiently obvious that non-believers know fairly well what words like ' God ' mean, even if they do not know God. Thus it would be possible for a non-believer to say, for instance, ' The word " God " refers to an Almighty Being, who is love, and who controls the universe ' : and this would be correct.

Yet there is a sense of ' mean ' or ' understand ' to which philosophers pay little attention; and it is this to which believers refer when they stress the incomprehensibility of religious assertions to the outsider. A selfish philanderer might say carelessly that he was in love with some girl, and I might say to him : ' You don't know what " love " means.' In the sense of 'mean' which we have used previously, this is untrue : the philanderer can use the word ' love ' perfectly well. What I am suggesting, of course, is that he has never been in love, or never really loved anybody. Another way of saying this would be ' You don't know what love is.' Most of us have a strong prejudice that it is impossible to grasp the full significance of a word without having had something of the experiences to which it refers; and perhaps this prejudice, as stated in this way, is not wholly unjust. For words have an emotional or poetic meaning as well as a prose meaning : though a blind man might be able to use the word ' red ' as a prose symbol, it is unlikely that he would write good poems in which redness was a central concept.

Believers can, then, communicate the meaning of their words and assertions to non-believers in the sense that they can teach them how to use their terms. This is what the Catechism in the Church of England Prayer Book does. Such a process may be very useful : it may give the non-believer a framework on which to hang experiences which may follow later. To grasp their meaning in the second sense, however, involves first-hand experience; and there seems no doubt that believers are right in considering first-hand experience as the prime essential for belief. For it is the actual impact of the experiences which rouses the interests and emotions of people, and hence leads them towards the making of assertions and belief in those assertions. Perhaps this is only rather an arid way of saying what believers say, when they claim that the first essential is to learn how to experience God : what Christians say, for instance, when they claim that our first task is to obey Christ's imperative ' Follow me ', rather than to doubt and to reason. But there are occasions when the arid statements of philosophy have an important part to play. They may be only the prologue : but the drama cannot proceed without them.

CHAPTER IV

PRACTICAL CHOICE IN RELIGION

WE HAVE come a rather long way from the beginning of this book, when we described the choice of a religion as being primarily a commitment. Our object in trying to demolish any insecure basis for such commitment, and to sketch out a plan for a secure basis, was to ensure that the commitment should be a rational and a justifiable one. This is a philosophical objective: and since the conditions for rationality and justifiability of belief apply to all men, not only to philosophers, it is also a practical objective. But it is important to realize that a person who is, inevitably, committing himself to one way of life rather than another is in a different position from the philosopher who is, *qua* philosopher, not necessarily bound to commit himself in this way. The former has got to live: the latter has only got to think. The philosopher can legitimately end up by saying: ' So, you see, we don't really know: though perhaps something on the following lines, bearing in mind the logic of the situation, may possibly turn out in practice to be . . . .' The plain man has to go further: he has to say: ' Yes, I see all this, but as things stand I still have to take some line or other: I can't (logically) be neutral. Not that I can't *say* " We just don't know " : but that I can't *live* without choosing some assumption to live by, whether it is an assumption of belief or disbelief.'

In other words, the plain man needs not only the rationality which philosophers (when the situation is a philosophic one) can help him acquire, but also a kind of practical rationality which will help him meet the present situation as it stands. The importance of this practical rationality, a rationality of choosing, does nothing to discredit the work of the philosopher, but it extends beyond that work. In the same way a practical decision like ' Shall I bet on red or black? ' is only partially assisted by a due consideration of probability and the laws of chance : and a decision like ' Shall we build a space-ship and go to Mars? ' does not entirely depend on what scientists say about the habitability of Mars and the conditions of outer space. Obviously no one who did not take the theoretical work into account could decide rationally : but whereas the theoretical work is not immediately concerned with the practical decision, people are so concerned. They have to be : for the *milieu* of practical decision is not one we can avoid.

In the present instance the difference between the rationale of a theoretical programme and the rationale of practical decision is very plain. Our case has been, to put it briefly, that religious knowledge must take as its starting-point religious experience : that it is by means of such experience, and not by regarding religious assertions as explanations, or self-justified, or authoritative, that we can rationally enter the realm of religious belief. The existence of such experience and the fact that it can (logically) be organized in such a way as to give sense and truth to religious assertions is, so to speak, the ticket or pass-word by whose virtue Reason permits us to enter. As philosophers, our theoretical programme will naturally consist of enlarging religious experience and strengthening its logical structure, so that Reason will walk hand in hand with us in religion as she does in science, and not leave us after giving a hesitant permission to enter. But at present even the need for such a programme has not been agreed : and meanwhile practical decisions have still to be made. To know that religion is logically respectable, and to see why it is so, is essential if we are to enter upon it rationally : but it is not enough. There is no question of denying the importance of the programme, or of going back upon the logical features we have succeeded in elucidating : it is rather a matter of putting ourselves in a position of practical decision and not in the position of theoretical philosophy. It is as if we had to decide whether or not to take an umbrella on a walk : a long-term programme for the advancement of meteorology and the prediction of rain may be the only way of settling such decisions rationally for good and all, but meanwhile we still have to decide.

Religious experience, in the absence of such a programme, is to-day fragmentary; and however logically respectable it may be for religion as a whole, it is not logically compelling for any particular religion. But the absence of logical compulsion does not entail the absence of every sort of rationality. We have a choice : and the choice can be exercised wisely or unwisely, with prejudice or without it. In practice, our choice is limited : it would take up considerably more than a lifetime to investigate the structure of very many religions, and the experiences which underlie that structure. This may be regrettable, but it has to be faced. Nor does it prevent us from a rational assessment of the claims of any religion which is a live option for us—of Christianity, for example. Our assessment will be primarily an assessment of the genuineness and cogency of religious experience insofar as any particular religion is based on such experience, and of the validity of the structure which such experience has been made to bear. Thus we can decide, and decide rationally, whether there is good reason to think that (say) Jesus, St. Paul, St. John and others had illuminating and trustworthy experiences or not : whether or not, to put it crudely, they can be taken as ' experts ' in religious experience. And here commonly-discussed questions like ' Were they sane ? ', or ' Does what they say remind us of our own experiences? ', are important.

Such a method may seem primitive to the philosopher : but the methods of practical decision are often primitive—though none the less valid. To go back to our analogy with aesthetic experience, we may remember that we can make rational or irrational choices about what sort of music to listen to, or what books to buy, even though there is no united body of expert opinion. We consider what critics seem sensible and reliable, what traditions of aesthetic value seem based on genuine experience, and so on. Our criteria for decision here are quite down-to-earth and ordinary. Somebody might tell us that a play has certain qualities : we see it, and discover the qualities for ourselves : afterwards we quite properly decide to pay some attention to what that person says on subsequent occasions. After a good deal of hard work or trial and error, we may be lucky enough to discover a critic who seems to us to be right almost every time.

What we cannot rationally do is to dismiss the whole thing as nonsense. Once we come to think that there is enough experience that is genuine to suggest that the realm we are entering (the realm of aesthetic beauty or the realm of the supernatural) is real and not fictitious, then we are rationally bound to search out that experience ourselves and to adopt some practical attitude to beliefs which emerge from it: insofar, that is, as this realm and these beliefs are important to our lives—and religious beliefs plainly have such importance. It may be difficult to decide how the realm is populated and what its countryside really looks like: but if we accept that it is a real realm, then this difficulty can only spur us on to greater efforts.

Because we work inevitably under severe practical disadvantages, and cannot hope to cover all the ground ourselves, we naturally seek some authority: with a clear conscience, since we know at least that the realm which the authority claims to map is a real one, even if he has mapped it faultily. After due consideration we choose an authority: we accept it, not as we accept scientific experts whom we take to be right on every occasion, but primarily as a guide—a short cut, if you like, which will help us to gain religious experience and fit it to a structure of belief more quickly and efficiently. What sort of authority we choose will of course depend on how far, and in what directions, we consider it trustworthy. We might, for instance, believe in a very high degree of reliability in our authority, and join the Roman Catholic Church: or place a more general and flexible trust in the authority of the Church of England.

As a result of our practical decision we may, therefore, choose to commit ourselves to a specific religious framework. It is important to observe that this is not taking a leap in the dark, not simply acting as a result of some hunch or intuition, not throwing rationality out of the window. For not only do we now know, philosophically, that the supernatural is logically respectable: but also reason requires that we should adopt *some* framework to assist in our interpretation of the supernatural—just as reason requires that we should bet on *some* number, if we are going to play roulette at all, or spend our money on *some* gramophone record, if we want to learn about music. It is also important that the commitment need neither diminish our critical faculties nor hold us back from the full, whole-hearted engagement that religion demands. The man who bets on something does not necessarily become irrational about the chances of his bet succeeding: but he may still be emotionally involved in it The two pictures of Faith and Reason tend to mislead us here also. We often suppose that the whole-hearted engagement of Faith means putting Reason to sleep, and conversely that to use Reason as a pilot means keeping Faith battened down in the hold out of harm's way. But of course the conflict is unreal: they do different jobs. No doubt it is hard to be fully engaged and yet fully rational, emotionally involved and yet intellectually critical: but this is a practical or empirical difficulty, not a logical impasse.

Just as it may be reasonable to enter upon a specific framework of interpretation, so it may be reasonable to fit specific problems to that framework. We are now no longer in the timeless, non-decisive realm of pure philosophy: we have opted for a particular type of interpretation. This process is not only rational, but almost inevitable. If you decide to use a certain map (without necessarily trusting it fully, or ceasing to use your own eyes as well), you must inevitably interpret various natural features in accordance with the map, at least in some degree: otherwise you are not really *using* the map at all, but merely testing it. Testing various religions is an important task: but as we have noticed, we cannot complete it in a short life-time. So we use a map, which means giving a prima facie acceptance to what it tells us about the terrain. If we did not know that the terrain existed, we would hardly be persuaded of the existence of any features of it, however many maps marked those features; but once we do know, the situation is logically different.

Provided we can form some conception of God on the basis

of our own or other people's religious experience—and this proviso is all-important—then we can rationally interpret that conception in terms of the framework we had opted for : we can, as it were, follow it through on the map. Starting from scratch, we saw that to regard explanation, or self-justification, or authority, as logically basic for religious assertions could not give us a respectable entry into religion. Having already gained that entry via religious experience, however, our position is different. We can then, as I described above, rationally accept a specific religious authority : and this means that our own attitude to particular beliefs will depend largely on how much weight the authority attaches to them. Again, we can now see some sense in religious language which represents God as disclosing himself in the natural world, and which seems to regard him as a cause or explanation. Or we could see how, once we have made the practical choice of accepting a framework and an authority, once we have entered into the whole religious category of thought, the assertions within that category could in a sense be said to ' justify themselves ' : that is, our acceptance of them depends on our total acceptance of the category of thought.

To have accepted the authority, the map, the framework, the category of thought is, indeed, to have made a leap : though not an irrational leap, not a leap in the dark. We can always avoid making the leap, though a point may come when avoidance becomes more unreasonable than commitment. To use a partial parallel, it is rather as if we were faced for the first time with the possibility of heavier-than-air machines flying. We could always explain away the apparent success of these machines in familiar terms, which did not involve acceptance of the general possibility of overcoming gravity in this way. We could say, for instance, that whenever an aeroplane appeared to fly something else was really supporting it : perhaps an airship filled with gas and hidden above the clouds, keeping it up with very fine, almost invisible wires. But after a time it looks as if we are trying to save the situation at any cost : after a time it becomes more sensible to accept the new category, the novel possibility. Or again, some people believe that the phenomena at spiritualist seances—rocking tables, flying tambourines, and so on—are all due to trickery, invisible wires, unseen pressures, etc. But there comes a point at which it seems better to enlist a new range of causes, even though we may not understand them : better to start believing in spirits, or telekinesis, or something of the kind, even though such belief may not immediately be all that we could wish by way of explanation. Here again it must be stressed that the position is radically different once we have had real experience, or at least know that there is something to have real experience of. To say ' God did it ' is neither explanatory nor meaningful unless we have a conception of God : it would be like saying ' Spirits make the table rock ' if we had no idea of what spirits were like. It would be simply trying to make a word do duty for an explanation.

Anything I were to say about the choice between one particular religious sect and another, apart from the purely logical considerations above, would inevitably be prejudiced : that is a matter for the individual. On this subject there is still a shortage of logic and a surplus of propaganda. One would suspect, however, that the confusion between the two types of activity, between the *milieu* of logical clarification and the *milieu* of practical decision, is partly responsible for our failure to reach any sort of agreement on religious questions. Both *milieux* suffer from this confusion : it is as if people were trying to play two different games on the same board. Each game, properly understood, reinforces the other. Without logical clarification, no practical decision about religion can be rational : without practical decision, no logical clarification can be more than academic. The result is that we neither think effectively nor live decisively.

But the search for clarity and decision faces other difficulties. In the early part of this book we described the religious attitude to the world and its features : and throughout our discourse it has been evident that we have been relying upon the possibility of such an attitude, together with the experiences that arise from it, and trying to show how such experiences could be built into a satisfactory logical framework.

Even those who may enjoy such an attempt for its own sake, however, will appreciate that unless the attitude is adopted, and the experiences realized, the attempt is of purely academic interest. Its cash value will depend on the actualization of the attitude and experiences : otherwise it would have little more use than, say, a work on aesthetic philosophy at a time when a majority of people had no aesthetic experiences.

Unfortunately this parallel is a little too close for comfort. Neither the attitude nor the experiences are widespread in our society at the present time. Religious believers are very well aware of this, and different sects make a great many recommendations with the object of improving the situation : to which we must add recommendations made by those who are not whole-hearted in their support of any particular creed. We may be told to read the Bible, to go to church, to react to the glorious panoply of the starry heavens, to take mescalin, to meditate, to pray, and so on. It is plain that this problem is chiefly a problem for psychologists and sociologists : and it is to them that we should refer any question such as ' Why do we, in our society, find a religious attitude difficult to adopt? ' Though this is not a question for philosophers, however, it is possible that philosophy, as so often, can prepare the way for answering it, if only by removing the stumbling-blocks of false logic.

One would suspect that our difficulties arise partly from the sudden and considerable growth of our control over the natural world. This has increased our security by increasing our ability to adjust the natural world to our own ends; but it has simultaneously diminished the necessity of adjusting ourselves to the natural world, and has made it more difficult for us to approach it on equal terms, let alone to regard it in anything like an attitude of awe or worship. Industrialization, the existence of large, sprawling towns which contain a vast majority of the population, the tendency to exploit natural beauty and reduce it to a series of ' beauty spots ', and the necessity to live at high speed in order to cope with the complexities of artificial life are some obvious symptoms of this trend. Man has become immensely precocious in respect of his intellectual and tool-using ability; and by making more and more demands on his time and energy, such precocity has thrown his emotional and spiritual immaturity into sharper relief. People tend to live on a series of momentary thrills, and are unable to experience to the full feelings such as grief, patriotism, or satisfaction in work. Even in cultural creation and experience there is a kind of neurotic split between the whole-hearted but juvenile lowbrow art, music and literature, and the sophisticated but rarefied highbrow culture. In this way our experiences of personal relationship, of nature, and of works of art have become both limited and distorted.

This has limited our categories of thinking in a most disastrous fashion. We can think in the category of science : that is, we can approach things with a view to understanding and controlling matter. We can think in the category of common sense, with a view to immediate utility. We can think morally, though even this category is weakening. We can think aesthetically, though with increasing difficulty. We can think or react, more easily than anything else, in terms of pleasure, in terms of exploiting things. Thus, we can approach a table as scientists, and investigate its atomic structure. We can approach it as housewives, and see whether it is serviceable for laying the tea on. We can approach it as aesthetes, and consider it as an artistic creation. We can approach a person as psychologists, or as moralists, or simply in order to exploit him for our own purposes. What we cannot do is to approach things holistically : we cannot accept them, contemplate them, and lay ourselves open to whatever experiences such an attitude might give us. The feeling of power or aliveness which is akin to religion cannot make itself felt to somebody who, for one purpose or another, is exploiting or operating for his own ends.

We find this attitude difficult to understand and to learn precisely because we fail to see where it could lead us, because it seems pointless, and fails to give us something which our brains or desires can pursue step by step. Contemplation and religious experience are essentially opposed to pursuit, exploitation or intellectual mastery ; but they are also radically unlike the absorption of pleasure through the senses. So far, indeed, is this approach removed from our natural bent that we tend to regard it as absurd. The limitation of our categories of thought have made us an easy prey to bias. We tend to equate the word ' real ' with the word ' concrete ' or ' material ' : the word ' subjective ' is a word of dispraise : even ' imagination ' is used as equivalent to ' illusion '. We have an instinctive tendency to devalue the contemplative and perceptive side of our natures, and to regard any activities in which this side indulges as entertaining, enjoyable, perhaps even illuminating—but in the last resort, not serious.

To take an example, a good proportion of the Old Testament has considerable value as a guide to experience, and little value as scientific or historical fact. One might say that it teaches one how to look at the world in a religious light, how to experience the divine power within nature, how to increase one's ability to meet the full force of creation. It seems to me that this offers quite an adequate ' defence ' of the Old Testament, if a defence be needed. Yet to most people, the abandonment of much of the work as scientifically or historically true, to which we may perhaps add its abandonment as a source of the highest morality, seems to entail giving it up completely. The only alternative, in the popular view, is to say that it is ' just ' poetry, or ' just ' imaginative writing : and the implication of ' just ' is, of course, that it need not be taken seriously—certainly not as part of religion.

The higher religions, largely by becoming ' higher ', have hardly succeeded in checking this process. The more detached from the material world God is made out to be, the more dissociated from common features of our life, then the more difficult becomes the religious attitude. Compared with a primitive religion, whose believers experienced some part of God in almost every aspect of their existence, the God of the higher religions is impossibly rarefied. We have avoided polytheism and anthropomorphism, it seems, only at the cost of making God totally unreal to most people. To attempt then to ' bring God down ' to our daily life is unreal : as unreal as to persuade a son that his father is passionately concerned with all he does, when that father—if he exists at all—lives on the other side of the world. Our concept of God has become sophisticated too quickly. A more basic approach is needed: we must look for God—or, which is easier, for divinity—in the world. It is no use saying that things are sacred to God if we do not know God. As always, we have gone too fast for our experience to keep pace. We think we know when we do not know. It is more than likely that ninety per cent of ' God ' is our own invention: indeed, when we remember the immense difference between the gods of different religions, this must be true in many cases.

If religion is to survive, it must first recognize these facts, and then face its problems one by one. It must appreciate that the solution of moral problems, the effectiveness of ritual, the historical validity of Scripture, the acquisition of genuine religious experience, and the formulation of metaphysical beliefs are all complex, and require their own particular type of assistance from experts. It cannot expect to retain a tight, integrated organizational structure in face of these difficulties, for it is a structure built upon sand: a structure which the advancing waves of various expertises—natural science, psychology, and analytic philosophy in particular—will demolish, if not by a frontal assault, then by a by-passing movement which will no less spell eventual disaster. Religion needs a complete re-assessment, a radical overhaul. A temporary gain from any irrationalism which psychological or material insecurity forces upon us can in the long run do religion nothing but harm, by discrediting it still further when security and reason resume their proper functions. Nothing will permanently assist the survival of any church or creed, unless believers themselves are prepared to retrace their steps— much as a patient retraces the steps of his life when under psychoanalysis. It remains to be seen whether religious organizations are sufficiently flexible and confident to make a move of this kind.

BIBLIOGRAPHY

The following is a brief list of works which the reader might find useful in connection with the present book:

J. C. Flugel, *Man, Morals and Society* (Pelican Books)

H. and H. A. Frankfort, *Before Philosophy* (Pelican Books)

A. G. N. Flew (ed.), *New Essays in Philosophical Theology* (S.C.M. Press)

Basil Mitchell (ed.), *Faith and Logic* (Allen and Unwin)

A. Mackintyre (and others), *Metaphysical Belief* (S.C.M. Press)

John Wilson, *Language and the Pursuit of Truth* (C.U.P.)

John Wisdom, *Philosophy and Psychoanalysis* (Blackwell)

A. J. Ayer, *The Problem of Knowledge* (Pelican Books)

INDEX

BELL AND BAIN, LIMITED
PRINTERS   GLASGOW